THE BARCLAYS GUIDE TO

Managing Staff

for the Small Business

IAIN MAITLAND

BARCLAYS
Published by
BLACKWELL

Copyright © Iain Maitland 1991

First published 1991
First published in USA 1991

Basil Blackwell Ltd
108 Cowley Road, Oxford, OX4 1JF, UK

Basil Blackwell, Inc.
3 Cambridge Center
Cambridge, Massachusetts 02142, USA

British Library Cataloguing in Publication Data

A CIP catalogue record for this book is available from
the British Library

Library of Congress Cataloging in Publication Data

Maitland, Iain
The Barclays guide to managing staff for the small business / Iain Maitland.
p.   cm. – (Barclays small business series)

Includes bibliographical references and index.

ISBN 0–631–17482–6 (pbk.)
1. Personnel management–Great Britain.   2. Small business–Great Britain–Personnel
Management.
I. Title.   II. Series.
HF5549.2.G7M35 1991
658.3'03–dc20   90–39672 CIP

Typeset in 10½ on 12½pt Plantin
by Hope Services (Abingdon) Ltd
Printed in Great Britain by
T. J. Press Ltd, Padstow, Cornwall

Contents

Contents

To Tracey and Michael

Other books by Iain Maitland

Iain Maitland is the author of many business books including

Running a Successful Advertising Campaign (Telegraph Publications)
How to Win at Job Hunting (Business Books Ltd)
How to Win at Interviews (Business Books Ltd)
How to Buy and Run a Shop (Northcote House)

Foreword

The past five years have seen a significant growth in the number of small businesses in all sectors of industry in the UK. Unfortunately they have also seen an increase in the numbers of problems encountered by those businesses. Often the problems could have been avoided with the right help and advice.

Barclays, in association with Basil Blackwell, is producing this series of guides to give that help and advice. They are comprehensive and written in a straightforward way. Each one has been written by a specialist in the field, in conjunction with Barclays Bank, and drawing on our joint expertise in business to ensure that the advice given is appropriate.

With the aid of these guides the businessman or woman will be better prepared to face the many challenges ahead, and hopefully, will be better rewarded for their efforts.

George Cracknell
Director UK Business Sector
Barclays Bank plc

Preface

I have written this book for the owners and managers of small businesses who are planning either to employ staff for the first time or to expand their existing workforce. Taking on a newcomer inevitably creates many anxieties and uncertainties. How do we set about recruiting and selecting the right person for our firm? What terms and conditions of employment should be offered? How do we make the most of our employees? What shall we do when difficulties arise? What are our legal responsibilities to our staff? This book fully explores and answers these and many other questions, explaining how to manage staff successfully.

Each self-contained yet complementary chapter looks at a different aspect of managing staff. Practical, down-to-earth advice and suggestions are given. Potential problems are highlighted and worked through. Rules and regulations are examined and clearly detailed. The text is written in a friendly, concise style with many subheadings and bullet points for easy reference. Questions are regularly posed to recap on information given and a brief summary at the end of each chapter acts as a reminder of its key points.

Although the book is comprehensive and thorough, some readers will still want to learn more about a particular topic of special interest to them. More detailed texts on particular issues are therefore regularly referred to and there is also a list of recommended specialist further reading. Names and addresses of useful organizations are given in the Appendix.

For ease of writing, the personal pronoun 'he' is predominantly used throughout the text. Please accept this as a shortened version of 'he or she'.

To know more about the do's and don't's of managing staff, simply read on . . .

Iain Maitland

Acknowledgements

I wish to thank the following for their assistance: Tim Cornford (NFER – Nelson Publishing Company Ltd); J. B. M. Donnellan (Association of Independent Businesses); P. B. Dottridge (Central Office of the Industrial Tribunals, England and Wales); Neil Hubbard (Oracle Teletext Ltd); Colin Osborne (Employment Service); C. M. Van Schagen (Small Firms Service); Fiona Shipp and Deirdre Waterhouse (National Federation of Self Employed and Small Businesses Ltd); Elly Slocock (Wimpy International); and Cathy Smith (British Institute of Management). I also thank the Employment Department, London Chamber of Commerce and Industry and the Training Agency.

Note

The author and publisher would like to point out that the use of the masculine pronoun 'he' is not gender specific.

I

Calculating your staff needs

Outline

Small business owners and managers must think about their staff needs carefully if they are to recruit the right employees. This chapter details how this should be done. It looks at:

- assessing requirements
- job analysis
- the job description
- the person specification
- planning for the future

Employing unsuitable employees can lead to problems, such as:

- inadequate work performance;
- unacceptable conduct (for example, lateness and absences);
- conflict between staff;
- low morale;
- an unnecessarily high turnover of your workforce (for example, more resignations and dismissals).

If a business is understaffed, employees may be:

- overworked;
- under stress;
- resentful;
- unable to cope with work demands.

Problems will also exist if a business is overstaffed. This can result in:

- an excessive wage bill (perhaps making the business unviable);
- too many employees chasing too little work;
- insufficient opportunities for career development.

To avoid these types of problems you must employ the right staff in the right numbers. This is difficult to achieve. To be successful, you must approach recruitment in a thorough, analytical manner.

Assessing requirements

Every time a job vacancy exists you should consider all the options open to you. The job could:

- be scrapped;
- continue on a part-time basis;
- continue on a temporary basis;
- continue on a full-time basis.

Scrapping the job

Is the job really necessary? Has it played a part in the success of your business? More importantly, will it do so in the future? If not, think seriously about ending it and sharing out the duties amongst your other employees. They may be pleased to accept more responsibility and – if overtime is required – extra income. Such a course of action could also save you time and money. You will not have to attract, select, train and pay a new job holder.

However, always consider both sides of an option. What are the advantages? An employee anticipating promotion may be unhappy that the job has ceased to exist. Staff who accept extra work and overtime may be overstretched and become exhausted. The quality of their work performance may fall.

Continuing on a part-time basis

Is your business constantly busy or do you regularly have quiet mornings, afternoons or days? If so, why not employ part-timers (under 16 hours per week) to cover your busiest periods? They may bring enthusiasm and freshness to their work. In addition, you will often avoid many of the 'invisible costs' of employing full-time staff (such as national insurance and holiday pay). Do be aware of the problems of employing part-time employees though. For example, they may be out of touch with the day-to-day needs of an ever-changing business (see 'Communicating with staff').

Continuing on a temporary basis

Is your business seasonal? Do you have busy summers and quiet winters? When are the peaks and troughs of demand? Contemplate taking on temporary – or freelance – staff at busy times. Employing people in this way may release you from many, expensive obligations (such as holiday entitlement and pay). However, temporary staff may find it difficult to fit in and contribute fully as it will take time for them to become familiar with your business organization and methods. You may also find it hard to discipline such employees. Freelance, self-employed staff can be quite expensive too.

Continuing on a full-time basis

Does the job warrant a full-time position? Will an employee be occupied day in and day out? Will a full-timer contribute more to your business than a part-time or temporary employee? Bear in mind *all* the costs of full-time staff – wages, fringe benefits (for example, discounted goods, subsidized food and drink), invisible expenses (such as national insurance, holiday pay) and administration (including PAYE, Statutory Sick Pay, Statutory Maternity Pay). Is it worth it?

If it is, should the job continue as it is now? Are all the tasks relevant? Perhaps the job needs updating – some tasks dropped and others added? Think carefully.

Have you considered job-sharing? Two part-timers could share a full-time job. This can improve staff morale as some employees may prefer to work on a part-time basis (for example, those with young children to look after). It can also be efficient. Often one employee will cover for the other during periods of sickness, holidays or time off. With part-timers, you may also save some of those invisible costs of employing staff. There may be other financial benefits as well. The Employment Department currently runs a 'Jobshare' scheme whereby employers who split a full-time job into two part-time jobs may be eligible to receive the sum of £1,000 towards administrative costs. This is subject to various rules. The main ones are that the full-time job must have existed for 26 weeks or more and have been for at least 30 hours per week. The job should not have been vacant for more than 13 weeks before the employer applies for 'Jobshare'. The two part-time jobs must be for between 16 and 29 hours per week (the hours do not need to be equal) and should be taken by the unemployed or by employees under notice of redundancy. Contact the 'Employment Department' in Birmingham (see Appendix) for further information, a booklet 'Jobshare; How it Works for Employers' and an application form (JS 1A).

What about the problems of job-sharing? Take into account the increased paperwork and administration. You will need to watch both employees carefully, especially in the early days. Are they taking an equal share of the responsibility? Are they both doing their fair share of the work? Do they 'gel' well together? Are there any communication problems?

If the job is to continue in some capacity, you must decide whom to employ. Do you transfer or promote from within your existing workforce or recruit externally?

Internal recruitment

Internal transfer or promotion has many benefits. You should be aware of your employees' qualities and limitations. You may therefore find it easy to match the right person with the job. Similarly, an employee will know you, your business and your policies thus avoiding many of the settling-in problems you could face with a new recruit (see 'Induction'). He may also know the job well and require less training.

If you decide to fill the vacancy from within, be careful how you go about doing it. If you simply offer the job to an employee who you think is suitable, you may offend others who could have been interested. Always be open and fair. Tell everyone (see 'Communicating with staff'). Ideally, write to each employee about the job and how they should apply (see 'Assessing and shortlisting').

External recruitment

Generally, this should be the last resort. It is time-consuming. For example, you will need to decide where to advertise for staff. Is the local newspaper better than the radio? How do they compare with jobcentres or employment agencies (see 'Sources of recruitment')? You may have to draft your own adverts. How should they be designed? What information should be included (see 'Advertising vacancies')? You will need to deal with many applications, rejecting some applicants and inviting others to an interview. You will have to select the right person (see 'Interviewing and selecting'). Once recruited, they must be trained. It all takes time.

It takes money too. Recruiting externally can be expensive. Advertising through many sources of recruitment is prohibitively costly. Various forms of training can be as well (see 'Planning a training programme').

External recruitment may also be risky. You know the strengths and weaknesses of your present employees because you see them at work every day, but how do you judge an external applicant? As indicated, if you make the wrong choice it can prove disastrous. Is it worth the risks?

If you do decide to recruit from outside your present workforce, it would be wise to tell your staff about the vacancy even if you do not think any of them are suitable. They – or their friends – may wish to apply. You will offend and upset them if they are not told and subsequently see the job advertised somewhere.

When assessing requirements, you therefore need to ask yourself these questions:

- Is the job required?
- Should it be streamlined on to a part-time basis?
- Could it continue on a temporary basis?
- Should it remain as a full-time job?
- Do the tasks need to be amended in any way?
- Have I thought about job-sharing?
- Could I transfer or promote from within?
- Should I recruit new employees?

To answer these questions, you really need to consider the job in detail, the type of person required to do it well and your future organizational needs. This process consists of:

- Analysing the job.
- Drawing up a job description.

- Drafting a person specification.
- Thinking about your future needs.

Job analysis

Before you can make any decisions, you need to know the job really well. Study it from every angle. Think about the following questions:

- What is the job title?
- Where is the job located?
- What is its purpose?
- Who does the employee answer to?
- Who is the employee in charge of?
- Who does he deal with in the course of his work?
- What are the main tasks of the job?
- How are those tasks completed?
- What work standards are expected?
- What skills, knowledge and experience are required to meet those standards?
- How much effort is required to do the job?
- Is it physically and/or mentally demanding?
- Which tasks are easy?
- Which tasks are difficult?

Most – or even all – of these questions can be answered by you. To get the fullest possible picture though, you must talk to other employees in the same (or similar) jobs, they may tell you about problems you never knew existed. You should also speak to the employee who is leaving – always conduct an 'exit' interview to see why he is going, what he thought of the job and what he liked and disliked about it (see 'Handling resignations'). Also listen to what the employee's immediate superior has to say.

You should then watch the job being done, perhaps even try it yourself to gain 'hands on' experience, and study your business records. Staff assessment notes or personnel records may shed new light on certain aspects of the job. In short – know the job as if it were your own.

For further reading on this topic, you should obtain the Advisory,

Conciliation and Arbitration Services' booklet 'Job Evaluation'. Refer to the Appendix for the address of your nearest ACAS office.

The job description

The information obtained from analysing the job should allow you to draw up a job description. This is a statement detailing:

- the job title;
- the job title of the employee's superior;
- the job title(s) of the employee's subordinates;
- the purpose of the job;
- the main tasks of the job.

Exhibit 1.1 is an example of a job description for an office assistant and exhibit 1.2 is for a sales representative.

A job description serves many purposes. It can help you:

- draw up a person specification;
- draft job adverts;
- plan out an application form;
- pre-screen applicants;
- assess candidates during interviews;
- teach new recruits about the job during induction;
- assess employees during staff appraisal;
- compare jobs (for equal pay and terms).

Draw up a job description carefully. You should:

- make it as accurate as possible so the employee knows what is expected of him;
- add a phrase such as 'the job holder will complete any other tasks requested' (to avoid subsequent disputes about what he should or should not be doing);
- avoid putting names on job descriptions as people often change jobs. Put their job titles instead.

```
                        JOB DESCRIPTION


    JOB TITLE:          Office Assistant


    RESPONSIBLE TO:     Office Manager


    RESPONSIBLE FOR:    _____


    PURPOSE:            To assist the Office Manager as required.


    TASKS:              To distribute incoming correspondence to
                        the appropriate person or department.

                        To photocopy and file copies of incoming
                        correspondence.

                        To type correspondence as instructed.

                        To dispatch outgoing correspondence.

                        To photocopy and file copies of outgoing
                        correspondence.

                        To maintain office stationery supplies.

                        To keep the office tidy.

                        To run errands as directed.

                        To carry out any other duties as instructed
                        by the Office Manager.


    PREPARED BY _____
    DATE _____
```

Exhibit 1.1 A job description for an office assistant.

```
┌─────────────────────────────────────────────────────────┐
│                     JOB DESCRIPTION                       │
│                                                           │
│                                                           │
│   JOB TITLE:           Sales Representative               │
│                                                           │
│                                                           │
│   RESPONSIBLE TO:      Sales Manager                      │
│                                                           │
│                                                           │
│   RESPONSIBLE FOR:     _____                   │
│                                                           │
│                                                           │
│   PURPOSE:             To maximize sales of nursery goods.│
│                                                           │
│                                                           │
│   TASKS:               To call on existing customers      │
│                        every month to obtain sales orders.│
│                                                           │
│                        To call on potential customers to  │
│                        obtain sales orders.               │
│                                                           │
│                        To submit sales orders as          │
│                        instructed.                        │
│                                                           │
│                        To maintain sales records.         │
│                                                           │
│                        To attend sales meetings as        │
│                        required.                          │
│                                                           │
│                        To complete any other tasks as     │
│                        directed by the Sales Manager.     │
│                                                           │
│   PREPARED BY _____             │
│   DATE _____                    │
└─────────────────────────────────────────────────────────┘
```

Exhibit 1.2 A job description for a sales representative.

The person specification

This is a statement – sometimes known as a 'job' or 'personnel' specification – which details the type of person required. It will list the skills, knowledge and experience needed to do the job well.

The late Professor Alec Rodger – an eminent occupational psychologist – devised a 'seven-point plan' which is frequently used as the basis of a person specification. The seven points – along with the type of questions you should be asking yourself – are as follows:

Physical make-up

Think about the person's age, appearance, speech and health – eyesight, hearing etc. Consider sex, race, height and weight too – but refer to 'Avoiding discrimination' first.

Attainments

What qualifications, training, previous experience, knowledge and skills are necessary?

General intelligence

How intelligent should he be – most employees will need to learn quickly and have a good memory and common sense.

Aptitudes

Should he have any particular inborn talents? Perhaps a head for figures, an artistic flair or 'green fingers'?

Interests

Would it be beneficial to have any particular sporting, literary or artistic interests?

Disposition

Should he have a particular temperament?

Circumstances

Does he need to live in a certain area, have a telephone, a clean driving licence or his own transport?

A person specification can help you:

- design adverts;
- assess applicants when they submit their applications;
- assess candidates during interviews;
- appraise staff.

When drawing one up there are certain pitfalls you *must* avoid. Do not be *vague*. For example, phrases such as 'well educated' and 'good shorthand speeds' should be replaced by 'educated to degree level or equivalent' and 'a shorthand speed of 80 words per minute is required'. Everyone defines 'good', 'bad' etc. differently. Avoid listing *abstract qualities*. Large companies can afford to employ specialists to conduct tests on job candidates to assess such qualities as 'the ability to learn quickly' but you cannot, so you should simply detail those qualities you can measure easily, such as qualifications. Be careful not to *demand too much*. Setting many requirements may limit the number of people applying. Finally, beware of *discriminating* against particular groups. Be sure not to discriminate because of a person's sex, marital status or race – it is illegal, see p. 86.

Examples of person specifications for an office assistant and a sales representative are shown in exhibits 1.3 and 1.4.

Planning for the future

When you decide to recruit staff you must not only think about your immediate needs but also your future needs as well. For example, you may be looking for a new office assistant. If you anticipate the office manager retiring in two years and do not have an existing employee ear-marked to replace him, consider recruiting a person who will not only be a good office assistant now but who can also be groomed to take over from the office manager when he retires.

Plan recruitment on a long-term basis. Adhere to the following guidelines:

PERSON SPECIFICATION

JOB TITLE: Office Assistant

THE JOB HOLDER:

must have a clean and tidy appearance.

must have a friendly, outgoing nature.

must have 4 GCSE's ('C' grades or above),
preferably including English Language and
Mathematics.

must be able to type at 50 words
per minute.

should have previous office experience
if possible.

must be able to work occasionally in the
evenings and on Saturday mornings.

PREPARED BY _____
DATE _____

Exhibit 1.3 A person specification for an office assistant.

- Think about your existing workforce, their ages, skills, qualities and experience.
- Anticipate likely staff turnover in the next few years. Do you expect any retirements? What about resignations? Do you have replacements ready to transfer or promote?
- Consider your future business plans. Do you plan to expand to

PERSON SPECIFICATION

JOB TITLE: Sales Representative

THE JOB HOLDER:

must be of smart appearance.

must speak clearly without speech impediments.

should have previous sales experience if possible.

should have some knowledge of the nursery trade.

must have a telephone.

must reside in the Yorkshire area.

must have a clean driving licence.

PREPARED BY _____

DATE _____

Exhibit 1.4 A person specification for a sales representative.

contract? Do you expect any changes in your business policies? How will these affect staff requirements?

- Take account of external factors that may influence supply and demand. As examples, it is well documented that skills shortages will continue to exist in parts of the United Kingdom, the number of school leavers will fall dramatically in the 1990s, more women are returning to work after having children and many employees are seeking to retire earlier. How will these trends affect you?
- Calculate the workforce required for the future.

In short, recruit today's workforce for tomorrow's needs.

Key points

- When a job vacancy exists, the small business owner or manager should see it as an opportunity to study all the options open to him. He must carefully consider the advantages and disadvantages of ending the job, continuing with it on a part-time basis and so on.
- The pros and cons of internal transfer or promotion should be looked at in relation to those of external recruitment.
- To decide on the job's future and – if it is to continue – the type of person needed, the job must be analysed from all angles. In turn, a job description and person specification should be drawn up.
- It is always wise to assess future staff requirements when reaching recruitment decisions. Take on employees who are suitable for both present *and* future jobs.

2

Recruiting staff

Outline

It is vitally important to know how to recruit employees successfully. This chapter fully considers and explains:

- sources of recruitment;
- advertising vacancies;
- assessing and shortlisting;
- interviewing and selecting;
- offers of employment;
- accepting the job offer.

Sources of recruitment

There are many ways of recruiting new staff. Your aim must be to choose a source (or sources) which will reach the type of person you want to apply. As an example, you might successfully advertise a managerial vacancy in the window of the jobcentre but not on a students' noticeboard at the local college.

You must obtain a sufficient number of applicants. Advertising on local radio in the early hours of the morning when few suitable people will be listening may mean you need to re-advertise the vacancy. This could cost you more time and money. You do not, however, want too many applicants to apply. A series of large adverts in all local papers could lead to hundreds applying for just one job. Reading and replying to so many applications is time-consuming and expensive.

Think about the cost of using a particular source of recruitment. Compare this expense with the type and number of persons reached. Adverts in national newspapers may be seen by a suitable number of ideal people but the cost of national advertising is prohibitive for a small business operating on a tight budget. At the same time, a postcard in a newsagent's window may be inexpensive but probably will not be seen by sufficient, suitable people.

In short, when considering the following sources of recruitment, always ask yourself one simple question: 'Will this source reach the right people in the right numbers at the right price?' If the answer is yes, think seriously about using it.

Local newspapers

Many towns and cities have their own daily and weekly newspapers which are read by a wide cross-section of the local population. Vacancies are often advertised in a special jobs section or supplement.

Advertisement rates vary depending upon the circulation of the newspaper and the required position of the advert. Cost is calculated 'per single column centimetre' (s.c.c.). To explain this briefly, a newspaper page is divided into columns. A typical page may have seven columns. An advert in one column would be paid for by the centimetre, that is, per single column centimetre. Usually a minimum of three single column centimetres must be purchased. Therefore, an advert in one column and three centimetres long charged at '£8 plus VAT per s.c.c.' would cost £24 plus VAT. An advert across two columns and eight centimetres long would – at the same rate – cost £128 plus VAT. (Note: 2.5 centimetres equals 1 inch.)

The cost of a single column centimetre is charged at a different rate throughout the newspaper. A 'classified' advertisement – which simply lists details line after line under a classified heading such as 'Situations Vacant' – might cost £6 plus VAT per s.c.c. in a typical local paper. A 'display' advertisement – which will have a border, probably a bold headline and different print – may cost £7 plus VAT. A 'semi display' advertisement – which is a display advert under a classified heading – could cost £8 plus VAT. Adverts can also be purchased in eighth-, quarter-, half- or full-page sizes. A full-page advert in a local paper could cost around £1,200 plus VAT, with other sizes at the appropriate, equivalent rate.

Advertising vacancies in local newspapers has many benefits, for example:

- extensive local readership;
- prompt publication (most local newspapers only require 48 hours' notice to place an advert);
- professional design and artwork services provided by the newspaper at no extra cost.

Newspapers do have limitations though:

- cost – there are many ways the small business can recruit staff successfully without any expense;
- wastage – many readers are not looking for work;
- unseen adverts – job seekers may not see your advert if it is hidden away amongst many similar ones;
- short life – a newspaper is often read quickly and then, with your advert, it is thrown away.

If you are interested in advertising in a local newspaper you should:

- Talk to other business people who have advertised in this way. Are they happy with the results?
- Obtain addresses of local newspapers from telephone directories, Yellow Pages or British Rate and Data (BRAD) (see Glossary).
- Study each local newspaper carefully to discover on which days vacancies are advertised and which type of advert you should choose.
- Contact the newspaper for a rate card, which usually details prices, deadlines and a post code breakdown of the circulation area with the numbers of households in each.
- Telephone the newspaper's advertisement department to discuss your plans (see 'Advertising vacancies').

Local radio

There are many small radio stations throughout the country which offer their listeners a mix of music, news and local information. Small businesses can advertise vacancies over a wide geographical area to different groups switching on at different times of the day and night.

Adverts are usually sold in packages. A radio station may offer a package of twenty-eight 30-second commercials to be broadcast at different, unspecified times of its transmitting day (6.00 am to 1.00 am) over a period of one week. The average cost of this package may be around £600 plus VAT (£21.43 plus VAT per commercial).

Packages are negotiable though. A sliding scale of prices for commercials of alternative duration is often available. For a series of commercials of 10, 20, 40, 50 or 60 seconds duration, expect to pay around 25 per cent more or less per 10 seconds. Therefore a series of twenty-eight, 20-second commercials over one week may cost £450 plus VAT (25 per cent less) whereas a series of 40-second commercials may cost £750 plus VAT (25 per cent more).

If requested, all adverts can be broadcast during the morning (6.00 am–1.00 pm) or afternoon/evening only (1.00 pm–1.00 am) at a typical cost of 50 per cent more or 25 per cent less respectively. A package could also cover Thursday, Friday and Saturday instead of the entire week at an extra 25 per cent. Discounts are available for repeating the package over consecutive weeks.

Single adverts can sometimes be booked for broadcasting at specific times of the day. A radio station usually divides its day (6.00 am–1.00 am) into five 3-hour segments and one 4-hour segment (9.00 pm–1.00 am) and the price of a single advert will be based upon the listening figures for each segment. Starting at 6.00 am–9.00 am and working through to 9.00 pm–1.00 am expect to pay around £60, £36, £24, £31, £19, £13 (all plus VAT) for one advert in the appropriate segment.

Radio stations also normally charge for writing and producing your advert (although you may be able to negotiate over this depending on the package purchased). An employment commercial with a jingle and one voice may cost around £25 plus VAT. Prices will increase for additional voices, sound effects and music.

Advantages of advertising on the radio include:

- adverts broadcast over a large area;
- specific groups listening at particular times of the day (for example, housewives in the morning, young people in the evening);
- prompt transmission – a radio advert can be produced and broadcast within hours;
- a professional production service (which will enhance your business image for all listeners, both potential recruits *and* customers).

There are also disadvantages to consider, however:

- cost – it is expensive in comparison with other sources of recruitment available locally.
- inattentiveness – listeners may not fully listen to the adverts, switching on just for the music or news.
- transience – your adverts only last for a short time and the listener may find it difficult to note or remember details.

If you plan to advertise on the radio you should:

- Discuss your ideas with other business people who have used it to advertise for staff. Does it work?
- Listen to the radio station – what do you think of the adverts they have produced? Are they good? Do they catch your attention?
- Find the address of the radio station from the telephone directory, Yellow Pages or BRAD.
- Write or telephone for a rate card which will provide information about the station's transmission area, total potential audience, estimated actual audience (divided into age, sex and class) and advertisement rates.
- Contact the sales or advertisement office for further information and advice.

Jobcentres

Located in many high streets, jobcentres offer a free recruitment service for employers and potential employees. Staff will take your job details and advertise the vacancy in their windows and on noticeboards within the centre. Details can also be circulated to other jobcentres if required.

When job seekers express interest in the vacancy, staff can immediately put them in touch with you or – if you prefer – can issue application forms and draw up a shortlist on your behalf. Suitable applicants can then be sent to you to interview or a room can be made available at the jobcentre if you would prefer to interview applicants there.

Jobcentres also provide free advice and information on other important employment issues such as training and employment law. For the small business, they are probably the most useful universal source of information on employing staff.

The advantages of using a jobcentre include:

- a free, simple-to-use source;
- adverts seen over a wide, local area by active job seekers;
- full assistance in the recruitment and selection process by quality, trained staff;
- help available in other employment areas.

However, there are disadvantages:

- staff do not always screen applicants well and unsuitable ones are sometimes sent to you;
- only active job seekers will see your adverts and apply whereas existing job holders may be interested if they knew about the vacancy;
- the quality and number of applicants may be reduced if only job seekers apply.

If you decide to use your local jobcentre:

- Obtain the address and phone number from your local telephone directory. It should be listed under Training Agency, Training Commission or Manpower Services Commission.
- Visit or telephone to give job details. Make sure staff know all about the job and the type of person you want, especially if they are to screen and shortlist for you.
- Supply copies of the job description and person specification.

Employment agencies

There are often a number of employment agencies in most towns. Some deal with vacancies for specific groups such as temporary or secretarial staff, others deal with all types of vacancies.

An agency will try to match your requirements with job seekers on their register. They may – if necessary – also advertise the vacancy in their window, in the local process or on local radio. Some even advertise vacancies on ITV and Channel 4's 'Oracle' teletext service. Most agencies also offer a screening and pre-selection service similar to the jobcentre.

Agency fees vary. If you are recruiting full-time staff, expect to pay around 10–20 per cent of the successful applicant's annual salary. For part-time staff you would be charged an appropriate, lower fee. For temporary staff, the agency will normally invoice you for the employee's services on an hourly, daily or weekly basis. The agency will then be responsible for paying the employee.

The benefits of using an employment agency to recruit staff are:

- they can be particularly good for recruiting specialist or temporary staff;
- a register of applicants may ensure prompt recruitment;
- assistance in pre-selecting applicants is generally offered.

The drawbacks are:

- it is expensive;
- agencies vary in quality and service offered;
- screening is sometimes inadequate and an unsuitable person is sent along.

The procedure for dealing with employment agencies should be as follows:

- Check whether other small businesses have found local employment agencies a good or bad source of recruitment.
- Obtain addresses and telephone numbers of agencies through Yellow Pages. Look under 'Employment agencies', 'Personnel consultants', or, if appropriate, 'Secretarial services'.
- Contact the agency to find out whether they specialize or deal with all vacancies.
- Discuss your requirements. Make sure they know exactly what the job involves, who you want and what you expect them to do (for example, issue application forms, interview for you). Supply a job description and person specification.
- Negotiate hard over the fee. Ensure a refund will be made if the employee proves unsuitable and resigns or is dismissed (for example, a full refund within one week, 50 per cent within one month and so on).
- Study any contract carefully before signing. Assess whether it is a fair deal. Seek professional advice if necessary.

Schools and colleges

If your business regularly needs a supply of young employees consider establishing close links with local schools and colleges. Creating a high profile for your business and industry may encourage many 'on spec' work enquiries from students and a prompt response when you advertise vacancies.

The advantages of approaching schools and colleges are:

- it involves little or no expense;
- there is a regular supply of young people looking for work;
- it is especially good for recruiting temporary, summer staff.

However, think about the disadvantages:

- young people often lack any previous work experience;
- they may find it difficult to adapt to working life;
- training can take longer.

If you think local schools and colleges are a good source of recruitment for your business, you should:

- Talk to business colleagues about recruiting young people. Ask them about the pros and cons.
- Obtain addresses and telephone numbers from your telephone directory or Yellow Pages.
- Contact the head teacher, careers officer or relevant department head.
- Supply your contact with regular information about your business to maintain a high profile throughout the school year. Send brochures, posters, press releases, catalogues, videos etc. You should also consider visiting and talking to students about your industry. Offering 'work experience' during holidays is a good idea too.
- Supply your contact with full job details when vacancies arise. Send adverts (see 'Advertising vacancies') for student notice-boards, magazines and distribution to class teachers.
- If you want to attract young people, you could also contact your local Careers Office, which provides careers advice for youngsters. Obtain the address and phone number from your local telephone directory. It may be listed under Careers Service or the name of

your local education authority. Follow the same procedure as for schools and colleges.

Word of mouth

When a job vacancy occurs you can simply tell everyone you know all about it and ask your staff to do the same. There are advantages in this method of recruitment:

- it is free;
- it may be quick and convenient;
- staff morale may be improved if friends and relatives are employed.

However, do be very wary of using this popular method of recruitment. There are many reasons for this:

- a mainly black or white workforce will tend to recommend friends or relatives of the same colour which may lead to claims of discrimination. Thus you should *never* use 'word of mouth' as a sole method of recruitment;
- friends and relatives are not necessarily the most suitable employees;
- cliques may form.

Teletext

The Oracle teletext facility available on ITV and Channel 4 offers local employers the opportunity to advertise for staff on a regional (or national) basis.

For regional advertising, the cost of a half-page advertisement for 3 months ranges from £460 (plus VAT) upwards depending on the television region used. A full-page advert for the same period commences at £840 (plus VAT). Discounts of 17.5 and 35 per cent are available for 6 and 12 months' advertising. (These figures are based on Oracle's July 1989 rate card.)

The advantages of using Oracle include:

- adverts seen right across the television region;
- immediate transmission (adverts can – in certain circumstances – be on air within minutes).

Consider the two main disadvantages though:

- it is more expensive than some other local sources of recruitment;
- only 27 per cent of households have a teletext set in 1989 (although this figure is rising steadily).

For a current rate card and further details write to or telephone Oracle Teletext Ltd at Craven House, 25–32 Marshall Street, London W1V 1LL (071-434 3121).

Whichever source (or sources) of recruitment you choose, always assess it at regular intervals to decide whether you should continue using it. There are five questions you should ask yourself.

- Are the right people applying?
- Are a sufficient number applying?
- Are too many applying?
- Is the source of recruitment cost-effective?
- Is it a success or failure?

Advertising vacancies

Once you have decided which source(s) of recruitment to use, you must think carefully about the way the vacancy should be advertised. Consider:

- What information should be put in the advert?
- How should that information be phrased?
- How should the advert be designed?

It is essential that you can answer these questions not only if you intend to draft your own adverts but also if others (such as a newspaper's advertisement department) are to do it on your behalf. You need to be able to assess the quality of their work.

Before planning your advert, you should first of all look at (or listen to) other adverts. Consider what details they include and exclude and in what way they put those details across. Which adverts do you think readers would respond to, and why? Then talk to the professionals. Find out what help and advice is available. Always listen to what other, more experienced people have to say. In the case of radio advertising, it is especially important that you not only talk to but are guided by the radio station's professional staff. By all means provide information and suggestions but this medium is so specialized that an amateur – however gifted – is unlikely to be able to plan and produce a good advert on his own.

Also, study again the job description and person specification. These documents provide all the basic information you need to include in the advert to ensure the job seeker can decide whether this is the job for him and he is the person for you.

The contents of an advert will always vary according to circumstances. For example, a display advert in a local newspaper may allow you more room than a notice in a jobcentre window. However, you would usually seek to include some – or even all – of the following details:

- The job title.
- The job location.
- Information about the business – the products you sell and/or the services you provide.
- Information about the job – its purpose and the main tasks.
- The job benefits – any benefits which will encourage people to apply for the job.
- The salary – always state the precise salary or possible range.
- The type of person required – the skills, qualifications and experience the right person must have.
- Who to apply to – yourself, a colleague or a subordinate.
- Where to apply.
- How to apply – whether by application form, curriculum vitae, letter or telephone.

The style and design of an advert will always vary too. Nevertheless, there are a number of universal guidelines which can be applied. An advert should be:

- eye-catching;
- interesting;
- brief;
- specific;
- well written;
- truthful;
- legal.

Eye-catching

Every advert should attract attention. It could have a bold headline – perhaps the job title if it sounds impressive or the name of your business if it has a good local image. (On the radio, a lively jingle or opening phrase could act as a 'headline'). Other ways of attracting attention include a strong border, different shades or styles of print, a company logo or an illustration. Colour or a large advert can also catch the eye, although do bear in mind the extra cost involved.

Interesting

Once the reader has seen the advert he must be encouraged to read it. What will interest him? Think about the type of person you want to apply. A sales representative would want to know about the products he would have to sell and the market position of your business whereas the office junior would be more interested in the type of office he would be working in and the equipment he would be using. All applicants will want to know about the salary, fringe benefits and prospects.

Brief

Few job seekers will read a lengthy, waffling advert. They will simply look at the advert next to it instead. Cut out all superfluous information. Use simple sentences and words to put your message across. Avoid technical phrases, slang or jargon: it puts people off.

Specific

You must try to limit the number of unsuitable people applying for the job. To do this you should always be precise. State exactly what the job involves and what your requirements are. For example, if you explain that a sales assistant's job also involves regular heavy lifting then those job seekers unwilling or unable to do this will not apply, saving you time and money in dealing with their applications.

It is also sensible to state the salary, or at least suggest a range. Some advertisers unwisely just indicate it will be 'attractive' or 'competitive'. Unfortunately, everyone defines these words differently. The result is that a large number of people may apply for the job but some will withdraw when they discover that the advertiser's idea of an 'attractive' salary is £5,000 per annum less than theirs. State what the salary will be and you will reduce the number of applicants and know that those who apply are happy with that figure.

Well written

Always check spelling and punctuation. They both play their part in the image the advert conveys of your business. Ensure the advert is also written in a logical order, dealing with one topic at a time.

Truthful

You need to create interest in the job but you must never exaggerate or lie. Misrepresenting the facts could lead to applicants subsequently withdrawing their applications. This could be both inconvenient and costly.

Legal

It is important that there is nothing in the way the advert is phrased that suggests only people of a particular sex, race or marital status may apply. Most sources of recruitment will advise you further on this but do remember it remains your responsibility to ensure your advert is non-discriminatory.

An example of a newspaper display advert is given in exhibit 2.1. This could easily be adapted for use in other sources of recruitment (such as jobcentres or employment agencies).

Assessing and shortlisting

You probably will not want to spend your valuable time interviewing every applicant, especially as some may be unsuitable and others only half interested (although it may – to maintain good staff relations – be prudent to offer all internal applicants an interview).

POTTERS PRAMS

require

OFFICE ASSISTANT

A vacancy now exists at our headquarters for an assistant to undertake a variety of duties in a small but busy office.

The successful applicant will be smart and friendly, able to type at 50 words per minute and have a minimum of 4 GCSE's (C Grade or above) preferably including English Language and Maths. Previous office experience would be desirable.

We offer the successful applicant a salary of £6,000 per annum, 21 days annual holiday, a 5 day week with occasional overtime and a friendly work environment.

For an application form, write to the Office Manager at Potters Prams Ltd, Brookland Road, Woodleigh, Sussex IP36 4HU

Exhibit 2.1 A newspaper advertisement.

An initial method of assessment can be used to eliminate many applicants and draw up a shortlist of perhaps six to interview. You can screen by:

- application form;
- curriculum vitae;
- letter;
- telephone.

Whether you intend to screen applicants yourself or employ a jobcentre or employment agency to do it on your behalf, you need to consider each method carefully. Which is most appropriate in your circumstances?

Application form

This most popular method of screening applicants has many advantages:

- it is a quick way of checking whether applicants meet your basic requirements as all information supplied will be in the same place;

28

- it is easy to compare applicants;
- useful, background information about the business, job and type of person required can be sent to applicants with the application form;
- you can check whether handwriting and spelling are satisfactory where these are important requirements of the job;
- the application form can act as a guideline in a subsequent interview (see 'Interviewing and selecting');
- the application form can serve as the basis of the successful applicant's personnel records (see 'Induction').

You should also consider the disadvantages of this method, however:

- it takes skill to draw up a suitable application form which asks the right questions;
- some applicants dislike lengthy application forms and a potentially ideal employee may decide not to apply.

If you choose to use this screening method you should seek advice and assistance from a jobcentre, employment agency or one of the other sources of advice listed at the end of this book. Also obtain and study as many different application forms as you can to see what questions are asked and how they are laid out. Then prepare an information pack (job description etc.) to be sent to applicants.

Base your application form on the person specification. Ask questions which will provide answers that allow you to judge whether applicants meet your requirements. Keep the application form as short as possible. Ask enough questions to help you quickly eliminate obviously unsuitable applicants, but remember asking too many questions is offputting. Always leave sufficient room for applicants to answer each question fully.

Streamline the application form to suit the job. For example, ask youngsters more questions about their education, qualifications and hobbies than about their work experience. They may not have worked before.

Ask applicants to complete the application form in black ink, which photocopies better than blue (you may want to let a colleague have a copy if you want his opinion about who to choose). Request applicants write in block capitals or type which may be easier to read

APPLICATION FOR EMPLOYMENT

PLEASE COMPLETE ALL SECTIONS IN YOUR OWN HANDWRITING. USE BLACK INK.

POSITION APPLIED FOR _____

FULL NAME _____

ADDRESS _____

_____

_____

TELEPHONE NUMBER _____

DATE OF BIRTH _____

EDUCATION (FROM THE AGE OF 11)

NAME AND ADDRESS

OF SCHOOL/COLLEGE/

UNIVERSITY   FROM   TO   EXAMINATIONS TAKEN   EXAMINATION RESULTS

EMPLOYMENT (COMMENCING WITH PRESENT OR LAST EMPLOYMENT)

EMPLOYER'S NAME AND ADDRESS	FROM	TO	JOB TITLE AND BRIEF DESCRIPTION OF DUTIES	SALARY	REASONS FOR LEAVING

LEISURE INTERESTS (TELL US ABOUT YOUR HOBBIES, MEMBERSHIP OF CLUBS AND SOCIETIES, POSTS OF RESPONSIBILITY ETC.)

COMMENTS (IS THERE ANY FURTHER INFORMATION YOU WISH TO SUPPLY WITH REGARD TO THIS APPLICATION?)

REFERENCES (PLEASE PROVIDE THE NAMES AND ADDRESSES OF TWO REFEREES, INCLUDING – IF APPROPRIATE – YOUR CURRENT OR LAST EMPLOYER. YOUR PRESENT EMPLOYER WILL NOT BE APPROACHED UNTIL AFTER AN OFFER OF EMPLOYMENT HAS BEEN MADE AND PERMISSION TO APPROACH THEM HAS BEEN GIVEN BY YOU)

NAME _____
POSITION _____
ADDRESS _____
_____
_____
_____

NAME _____
POSITION _____
ADDRESS _____
_____
_____
_____

I CONFIRM THAT TO THE BEST OF MY KNOWLEDGE ALL INFORMATION GIVEN IS CORRECT.

SIGNATURE _____   Date _____

Exhibit 2.2   A basic application form.

than handwriting (unless, of course, you particularly want to study their handwriting).

Be careful to avoid asking questions which may be (or appear to be) discriminatory. Questions about nationality, marital status or the number and ages of dependants should generally be avoided.

Request the names and addresses of two referees (you do not want to waste time in an interview noting this information). Make sure you state that a current employer will *not* be approached until after a job offer has been made *and* permission to approach them has been granted by the applicant. (Otherwise he may be reluctant to complete this section in case his present employer finds out he is job hunting.) Exhibit 2.2 is a condensed example of a basic application form. Do leave lots more room than is shown!

Curriculum vitae

Some employers ask applicants to send in their curriculum vitae, or 'CV'. There are benefits in using this method:

- A well-written CV will usually provide full details about the applicant in a logical order.
- It should be quick and easy to check from the CV whether basic requirements are met.
- A CV can be used as the basis of an interview (see 'Interviewing and selecting').

However, there are drawbacks too:

- Some applicants do not know how to compile a CV in the correct manner and a potentially good employee may slip through the net.
- Unless your advert was very specific, applicants may not know what your requirements are and may not supply you with the information you need to screen properly.

Letter

Asking applicants to apply in writing is another initial method of assessment which remains universally popular. Consider the advantages:

- You can check and assess applicants' handwriting, spelling and style of writing.
- It is a particularly useful method if you expect many people to apply as you can screen by letter and then ask a selected number to complete an application form.
- It may be less time-consuming than drawing up and sending application forms or talking on the telephone.

Think about the disadvantages as well:

- Some people may be poor letter writers but could be good at the job (for example, a salesman is rarely employed for his ability to write a good letter).
- It may be difficult to find the information you require, especially if a letter is long and rambling.

Telephone

There are several reasons to consider using the telephone to screen interested applicants:

- It is a quick and informal method of assessment.
- It reduces paperwork and administration.
- It is a good way of assessing an applicant's speech and ability to converse. These may be important qualities detailed in the person specification.
- The inclusion of a telephone number often increases the number of applications.

Think about the disadvantages though:

- More applicants means more work for you.
- The phone will ring at all hours of the day, which may be inconvenient.
- It can be hard to assess each applicant fairly. You could be conned by a sweet talker who cannot actually do the job very well.
- Some applicants may be unable to telephone during normal office hours, especially if they already have a full-time job.
- You may find it difficult to talk on the telephone if you are shy or an inexperienced interviewer.

If you decide to use the telephone to screen applicants, you must ensure you have plenty of time to deal with incoming calls (or assign an assistant to do the initial screening for you). Prepare a list of questions to ask all applicants (see 'Interviewing and selecting') and compare the applicants' answers to the person specification (see page 10). You should be reluctant to reject an applicant over the telephone. You may become involved in an argument if the applicant demands to know why and then tries to convince you that you are wrong. Some people refuse to take 'No' for an answer. Say you will be in touch ('I've other applicants to consider etc.') and send a letter of rejection based on the example in exhibit 2.4.

Ask the applicant to provide further details in a letter or curriculum vitae if you are in doubt. After all, a person may be nervous about talking on the telephone but this may not necessarily mean he could not do the job well. If the applicant appears potentially suitable invite him to an interview. Agree a time, place and date and follow this up with a letter of confirmation. Base this on the example given in exhibit 2.5.

Dear _____

Thank you for your completed application form/curriculum vitae/letter regarding the post of _____
This is currently receiving our attention and we will be in touch with you again shortly.

Yours sincerely

A. Reynolds
Office Manager

Exhibit 2.3 A letter acknowledging a job application.

If you assess and shortlist by one of the other methods discussed, there is a basic procedure you should follow. On receipt of the application form, CV or letter, send a brief letter of acknowledgement (see exhibit 2.3). This is common courtesy *and* good public relations. Applicants may be customers too so it is important they always have a good impression of your business. Compare the application carefully with the person specification and assess whether the applicant matches your basic requirements. Is he suitable? Should you now reject or invite him to an interview?

If you decide to reject, send a letter of rejection (see exhibit 2.4). Do this promptly and make the letter as pleasant as possible to maintain a good business image. Generally, do not explain *why* you are rejecting; this may lead to ill feeling and further correspondence. As indicated, some rejected applicants can be very persistent if given the opportunity.

Dear _____

Thank you for your completed application form/curriculum vitae/letter regarding the post of _____

We have considered your application carefully but regret to inform you that on this occasion you have not been successful.

We would, however, like to take this opportunity to thank you for your interest and wish you every success for the future.

Yours sincerely

A. Reynolds
Office Manager

Exhibit 2.4 A letter rejecting a job application.

Make a careful note of why you rejected the applicant. Keep this, along with the original application, your acknowledgement, letter of rejection and any other correspondence, on file for three months. This is the period of time during which rejected applicants can apply to an industrial tribunal on the grounds of discrimination during the selection process (see 'Avoiding discrimination' and 'Industrial tribunals').

If you decide to invite the applicant to meet you, it is sensible to telephone (if possible) to arrange a date, time and place. Some employers write instructing applicants to arrive at a certain time on a particular day. Not only does this appear rather rude but some applicants may not be available when you want to see them (for example, many applicants may already be working and will need to ask for time off – see 'Holidays and time off'). In addition, unexpected postal delays may mean your letters do not arrive on time.

Having telephoned and arranged a mutually convenient time, send the applicant a letter confirming your name (or the name of the interviewer if it will not be you) and the time, place, date and length of the interview. You could also supply a map (if you think your premises are hard to find) plus some information about the job and your business. If you want the applicant to bring work samples or proof of qualifications mention these in the letter as well. An example of a letter inviting an applicant to meet you is shown in exhibit 2.5.

Interviewing and selecting

An interview has three basic aims, which are:

- to enable you to assess whether a candidate is the right person for the job;
- to allow the candidate to decide if this is the right job for him;
- to promote an image of a good, caring business (so that the right person will want to accept your job offer and rejected candidates will still think highly of your business).

To achieve these aims, you must know how to prepare for, conduct and assess an interview.

Preparing for the interview

First, you must decide how you will interview candidates. Consider the following methods.

Dear _____

Thank you for your completed application form/curriculum vitae/letter regarding the post of _____

Further to our telephone conversation of _____, I write to confirm you are invited to attend an interview at (time) on (date) at (location). This interview will last approximately _____ minutes and will be conducted by myself. Any travelling expenses incurred in order to attend the interview will be reimbursed.

I enclose a map on which I have highlighted the location of our premises. I also enclose some literature about our business and the job, which you may find interesting.

I look forward to meeting you.

Yours sincerely

A. Reynolds
Office Manager
Encs

Exhibit 2.5 A letter inviting a job applicant to an interview.

The 'one-to-one' interview

You – and you alone – can simply interview each candidate on a one-to-one basis. This has many advantages:

- it is easy to arrange a date, time and place convenient to you both;
- it is fairly informal;
- the candidate will feel more relaxed facing only one interviewer and is therefore more likely to reveal his 'true colours' than if he is tense and nervous;
- it is easier for the interviewer to control and lead the conversation in the right direction.

You should consider the disadvantages too:

- it can be an unreliable method of assessment (for example, you may – perhaps unconsciously – be biased against certain types of people which could affect your selection of the right person);

- you could be a poor interviewer, unable to assess whether candidates are suitable for the job;
- you may be inexperienced at interviewing and find it difficut to reach a decision on your own.

The 'panel' interview

An increasingly popular method of interviewing is to have a panel of two or more interviewers. In a small business, the panel could consist of you, the successful candidate's direct superior and, if the job is specialized, an expert in that particular field (so that a candidate's knowledge and previous experience of the job can be accurately assessed).

The panel interview has many advantages over the one-to-one interview:

- it is a fairer, more accurate method of assessment as it is unlikely that every interviewer will be biased against a particular candidate;
- interviewers can share the responsibility of asking questions and making the selection decision;
- it can be less stressful for the inexperienced interviewer;
- it may appear more impressive and business-like;
- it is easier to make notes about a candidate without breaking up the flow of conversation (see page 44).

There are disadvantages though:

- it can be tense and nerve-wracking for a candidate to have to face several interviewers;
- it may be difficult to get all the interviewers (and candidates) together at the same time;
- there could be tensions between interviewers with one perhaps trying to dominate.

Once you have decided *how* to interview candidates, you must then think about *where* you will interview them. Choose a quiet office (or room) where you will be able to concentrate without noise from adjacent offices, the telephone ringing or colleagues wanting to speak to you. In addition, make sure there are no distractions in the office. For example, ensure the candidate has a comfortable chair, the sun is not in his eyes and your desk is clear of books and files. These – apparently minor – points can all adversely affect a candidate's concentration. For an interview to be successful, both the candidate and the interviewer(s) need to be able to concentrate totally. Remember if you do not have a quiet office in which to interview candidates, you can use an interview room at your local jobcentre, see 'Sources of recruitment'.

Every interview should be planned. You must decide which topics you want to discuss and what questions you need to ask in order to assess whether the candidate is the right person. Prior to the interview read through the relevant documents again:

- The job description. What job-related topics do you need to cover? For example, do you want to talk about a candidate's previous work experience to see how closely it matches the work involved in this job?
- The person specification. Think about the type of person you are looking for. What topics and questions will help you to decide whether a candidate is suitable?
- The candidate's application form/CV/letter. What facts do you need to check? Are there any gaps or anomalies you must mention? Make a note of particular questions you should ask.

Planning topics and questions will help you to guide the interview and ensure you cover all the relevant points. However, at the same time, you must be flexible during an interview. Do not adhere rigidly to your notes suddenly moving from one topic to another after a set number of questions. You must always be prepared to 'go with the flow', picking up and developing comments made and exploring new areas as they arise. Remember, an interview plan should be used as a guide and a checklist – not as a set of pre-determined questions that must be asked one after the other. Examples of the type of topics and questions you might ask a candidate are given on page 42.

Take the documents with you into each interview. They may remind you of the areas you want to cover. The person specification can be used as an assessment form – you can tick off requirements as they appear to be met and jot down notes on it about the candidate (to refresh your memory after the interview). The application form,

CV or letter may also be especially useful. Many interviewers loosely base their interview plan on a candidate's application, working through it and asking questions about each section in turn.

Finally, decide who will greet candidates as they arrive. Ideally, you should do this but if it is not possible (perhaps because you are interviewing) ensure a colleague or an employee is assigned the task. Never leave candidates to wander aimlessly about. It is ill mannered and a potentially suitable employee may decide he does not want to work for a business which treats him in such a cavalier fashion.

Your colleague (or employee) should greet each candidate with a warm smile and 'Hello. Welcome to ——'. If the candidate has to wait, he should be shown a seat and offered a drink (tea/coffee) and company literature (brochures/catalogues) to read. If travelling expenses are being paid, these could be dealt with at this stage too.

Conducting the interview

Open each interview by putting the interviewee at ease as quickly as possible. A relaxed interviewee will normally reveal more about himself than a tense one. Adhere to the following rules:

- Try not to keep him waiting. If you do, it will increase tension and may appear rude – especially if you do not apologize.
- Greet him with a smile and a firm handshake. Say, for example, 'Hello, Mr ——. My name's Tony Reynolds. I'm pleased to meet you.'
- Lead him to the interview room, making polite and pleasant conversation ('Did you have a good journey? Were we easy to find?').
- If appropriate, introduce him to the other interviewers, explaining their position in the business ('Mrs Barham runs the sales office') and their role in the interview ('She'll be telling you about the job and asking you about your previous work experience.').
- Show him to his seat. Some interviewers suggest you should offer a sweet or drink at this stage as these can help the interviewee to relax. Try to avoid doing this though. At best, food and drink are unnecessary distractions; at worst, they can be embarrassing. The interviewee will find it difficult to eat, drink and talk at the same time. He may choke on a sweet, or spill a drink.

- Start the interview by talking about the business (its products, services, customers, the market), and the type of person required. This will give the interviewee time to settle, assess you and relax.

When the interviewee appears to be relaxing, you can move on to the topics and questions you wish to raise.

Personal details

Tell me about yourself. What do you do in your free time? Do you have any hobbies? Tell me about them. Are you a member of any clubs or societies? Use pleasant, friendly questions such as these to start a conversation. If the interviewee appears excessively nervous, begin by asking simple, fact-checking questions, such as: Where do you live? What school did you go to? How many 'O' levels/GCSE's do you have?

Education, qualifications and training

Tell me about the school/college you attended. What did you like/ dislike about it? What did you think of your tutors? Did you hold any positions of responsibility? What qualifications do you have? Why did you study those subjects? Tell me about your training. Have you attended any special courses?

Work experience

Tell me about your work experience. What do you do in an average day at work? What do you like about your present/last job? What do you dislike? What are you responsible for? What do you think of your boss/colleagues/subordinates? Do you work on your own or in a team? Which do you prefer?

Plans and ambitions

Why do you want this job? What can you offer us? What are your strengths? Do you have any shortcomings? What are your ambitions? Where do you want to be in five years? Tell me about your long-term goals.

Of course, there are many other topics and questions you can cover. It's up to you to decide the content and order of each interview depending on circumstances. Do remember to be flexible though.

Whatever questions you ask during an interview, you should think about the way they are phrased. It is important that you can differentiate between several types of question.

Open questions begin with words such as 'what', 'how' and 'why'. For example: 'What made you apply for this job?' and 'Why did you choose to go to that university?' These questions give the interviewee the opportunity to talk and express ideas and opinions. Ask open questions as often as possible. They will help you find out more about the interviewee.

Closed questions are those which produce a 'yes' or 'no' answer. For example: 'Did you get three 'C' grade 'A' levels?' and 'Are you over 18?' These questions are useful if you want to check basic facts or keep the conversation going with a nervous interviewee.

Limited questions commence with words such as 'who', 'where', 'which' and 'when'. For example: 'Who do you work for?' and 'Which school do you attend?' Similar to closed questions, these can be used to establish facts and keep the conversation moving.

Leading questions indicate the answer that should be given. As an example: 'I want a hard-working employee. Are you hard-working?' The answer reveals nothing to you about the interviewee because you have effectively told him what to say. Avoid leading questions.

Hypothetical questions beginning with phrases such as 'What would you do if . . . ?' and 'How would you deal with . . . ?' may help you to assess how the interviewee would respond in the work environment. Make sure such questions are strictly relevant though. Think about the types of situation that could arise in a typical day (customers complaining, damaged goods delivered etc.) and ask the interviewee what he would do in those circumstances. (Don't forget that the answers will be hypothetical too and the interviewee may not actually react in the manner suggested.)

Multiple questions, such as 'What do you do in your free time, do you have any hobbies or belong to any clubs or societies?' can be confusing. The interviewee does not know which part to answer first. Avoid asking such questions.

During the interview you should adhere to a number of simple tips which will ensure it runs smoothly. Consider the following:

- Keep an open mind. Never make a decision in the first few minutes based on the interviewee's appearance, speech or mannerisms and then spend the rest of the interview trying to substantiate it. Avoid gut feelings or hunches – they are often wrong. Give all interviewees a fair and equal hearing (see 'Avoiding discrimination').

- Avoid talking too much. You must obviously talk about the business and the job so the interviewee can decide if this is the job for him. You will also probably need to speak more if he is young, inexperienced and/or nervous. Nevertheless, do remember that you want to find out whether he is suitable for the job and you should therefore listen to what he says.

- Encourage the interviewee to talk. Use more open than closed or limited questions – except for when you are checking basic facts on the application form, CV or letter.

- Appear interested at all times. Smile and nod as he speaks and use encouraging phrases such as 'Go on . . . ', 'That's interesting . . . ', 'Tell me more . . . '.

- Do not let the interviewee ramble or meander haphazardly. Bring him back to the question or lead on to the next topic with phrases such as 'Can we come back to . . . ', 'Tell me more about . . . ', 'I'd like to look further at . . . ' and 'Let's move on to . . . '.

- Make notes. You cannot expect to remember everything about each candidate, so take notes. Be open and tell him what you are doing. Be careful not to break the flow of conversation by writing excessively. Avoid writing immediately after the interviewee has given you potentially detrimental information – 'I was dismissed . . . ' – as this may affect his confidence. Keep an open mind and listen to his explanation. Then make a note.

Towards the end of the interview – when you have covered all the necessary topics – you should give the interviewee the opportunity to ask you questions. He will probably want to know more about the job, perhaps picking up on information given in job advertisements (see page 24), literature sent with the invitation to an interview (see page 37) or during the interview itself. He could also ask you about other terms and conditions not previously mentioned.

See this as an opportunity to fill in any gaps. Answer his questions fully and honestly, highlighting both good and bad aspects of the job. You certainly do not want him to accept your subsequent job offer, start work and then resign a month later because it was not what he expected. You will have to start the recruitment process again. Make sure he knows what is involved now.

Draw the interview to a close by thanking the interviewee for coming and telling him what happens next. Do not offer him the job there and then even if you think he is suitable. A subsequent interviewee may prove to be more suitable. Similarly, do not reject him even if he is clearly unsuitable. You may become involved in a discussion or an argument as he tries to convince you that you are wrong. Other interviewees may be waiting to see you. It is sensible to perhaps say 'Thank you very much for coming in. I'll be in touch within the next few days.' This will then give you time to see other interviewees, compare each one and reach a definite decision.

Signal the interview is over by standing up and shaking hands. Show him to the door. Smile, thank him again and say goodbye.

Assessing the interview

After all the interviews have been completed you must reach a decision. Which interviewee should be offered the job? In turn, read each interviewee's application form, CV or letter again. Look at the notes you made about him during his interview. Think about his interview performance. Compare him to the person specification. Imagine him actually doing the job. Who should you choose?

Is anyone suitable? If not, perhaps you are setting standards which are too high. Is your person specification too precise? Are the requirements really necessary? Be careful not to lower your sights too far though just to fill the vacancy. It is usually better to re-advertise – perhaps using different sources of recruitment – than take on an unsuitable employee.

Often, several interviewees could do the job well. If this is the case, think about your future needs. Which one is the best, long-term prospect? Who could move up and replace other employees as they are transferred, promoted or retired?

Once you have reached a decision you must then offer the job to the most suitable interviewee (see 'Offers of employment'). Keep one or two interviewees in reserve though just in case your first choice turns the offer down. Reject all the other interviewees (see page 49).

Offers of employment

An offer of employment can be made orally or put in writing. It is sensible to make a written offer (or at least follow an oral offer with written confirmation) as this will reduce the possibility of subsequent disagreements about the terms offered.

Your offer should include information about:

- the job title;
- the job location;
- the job title of the new employee's direct superior;
- the salary – amount, when paid, how paid, overtime rates;
- hours of work – per day, per week, lunch breaks;
- holidays;
- the trial period – you may feel it would be appropriate to offer the job on a trial basis for perhaps three months;
- the date when work will commence – this will normally be decided by mutual discussion and agreement;
- the conditions of the offer – it is usual to make a job offer subject to satisfactory references and perhaps a medical – although these are expensive for a small business to arrange and should not be demanded unless considered absolutely necessary.

An example of a written offer of employment is given in exhibit 2.6.

Always take up references to check facts and confirm your opinion that you have made the right choice. (Make sure a present employer is not approached until permission has been granted by the new employee.)

Ideally, references should be supplied by current or former employers and – for young people – school, college or university lecturers. Write to a referee asking questions about your (hopefully) new employee's

- length of service (or number of years at school, college or university);
- job (or subjects studied);

Dear _____

Further to your recent interview, I am pleased to offer you employment as a
_____ based at _____. You will be responsible to _____.

Your starting salary will be _____ per annum, paid monthly in arrears
into your bank account. Overtime will be paid at _____.

Your normal hours of work will be from _____ to _____, totalling _____
per week. You will be entitled to a one hour lunch break which must be
taken when convenient to _____.

You will also be entitled to _____ days paid hoiday per year (plus statutory
holidays). Our holiday year runs from _____ to _____.

Other terms of employment will be provided on your first day of work.

I would be grateful if you would confirm in writing if you wish to accept this
offer and when you will be able to commence work. Finally, can you also
confirm that I may approach your present employers for reference purposes.

I look forward to hearing from you.

Yours sincerely

A. Reynolds
Office Manager

Exhibit 2.6 A written offer of employment.

- ability;
- general conduct;
- honesty;
- time-keeping;
- health (as indicated, medicals are costly but you do want to be
  sure he will not be continually ill or off sick – you may therefore
  find his referees' comments on his track record to date are
  illuminating);
- reasons for leaving.

Also, ask previous employers whether they would re-employ him. Their answer may be revealing. An example of a letter to a previous employer is given in exhibit 2.7. Finally, you may prefer to talk to referees on the telephone as they will tend to give more information than in a written reply. If so, write first to establish your bona fides and to give them time to gather their thoughts and opinions.

Dear _____

Your name has been given to us as a referee by _____. As such, we would be grateful if you would be so kind as to answer the following questions. All information supplied will be in confidence.

– How long was _____ employed by you?
– In what capacity was he employed?
– How would you rate him in relation to his (a) ability to do the job (b) conduct (c) honesty (d) time-keeping (e) health.
– What was his reason for leaving your employment?
– Would you re-engage him?

A stamped, addressed envelope is enclosed. We thank you for your assistance.

Yours sincerely

A. Reynolds
Office Manager

Exhibit 2.7 A letter to a referee.

Accepting the job offer

Once your job offer has been accepted (and any conditions have been met), you should draw up a written statement of the main terms of employment for your new employee.

By law, a written statement must be given to employees who work for 16 hours or more each week (or who have worked for 8 hours per week for 5 years). It must be issued within 13 weeks of starting work.

The following information should be detailed in the written statement *or* in other, easily accessible documents – such as staff handbooks – to which reference must be made.

- The employer's name.
- The employee's name.
- The date employment commenced.
- The job title.
- The rate and intervals of pay.
- The normal hours of work.
- Holiday pay and entitlement.
- Sickness pay and arrangements.
- Pension arrangements.
- Disciplinary rules and procedures.
- Grievance and appeal rules and procedures.
- Notice period required by either party.

An example of a written statement is given in exhibit 2.8.

Draft two written statements for you and your new employee to sign. One is for him and the other is for your files. It is up to you when you issue him with his written statement (so long as it is within 13 weeks of starting work). You could perhaps wait until a trial period has been satisfactorily completed.

For further information on written statements read the Department of Employment's free booklet 'Written Statement of Main Terms and Conditions of Employment'. Contact your local office for a copy.

You also need to reject the other interviewees once your offer of employment has been accepted (you could, in fact, have rejected some interviewees earlier as long as you had kept one or two in reserve until now just in case your first choice had turned you down). Send rejection letters which are pleasant and friendly. Remember, rejected interviewees may be customers too. They could also be ideal for other jobs in the future (make a note if you think they may be). They will not apply if you have offended them. Try to avoid stating the reason for rejection. They may follow this up and try to prove you have made a mistake. An example of a letter of rejection is given in exhibit 2.9.

Keep application forms, interview notes, letters of rejection etc. on file for three months in case a rejected interviewee feels he was

STATEMENT OF EMPLOYMENT

Employer: _____

_____

_____

Employee: _____

_____

_____

Your employment commenced on _____.

You are employed as a _____ at _____.

Your pay is _____. This will be paid monthly in arrears into your bank account, commencing the 20th day of the month following the month you started work.

Your normal hours of work are ____.

Overtime will be paid at _____.

You are entitled to ____ days paid holiday – plus paid statutory holidays – each calendar year.

Sickness pay and arrangements are detailed in the staff handbook supplied with this written statement. A further copy is available for inspection in the staff restroom at any time.

We have no company pension scheme.

Disciplinary rules and procedures are detailed in the staff handbook.

Grievance and appeal rules and procedures are detailed in the staff handbook.

Notice to be given by the employer is _____.

Notice to be given by the employee is _____.

Signature of employer _____

Date _____

Signature of employee _____

Date _____

Exhibit 2.8 A written statement of the main terms of employment.

Dear _____

Thank you for attending the interview regarding our vacancy for a _____ .

We have given your application careful consideration but regret to inform you that we are unable to offer you this position.

We are sorry if this is a disappointment but hope you are successful in finding a suitable position soon.

Yours sincerely

A. Reynolds
Office Manager

Exhibit 2.9 A rejection letter following an interview.

unfairly treated and decides to apply to an industrial tribunal (see 'Industrial tribunals').

For further reading on recruiting staff, obtain the advisory booklet 'Recruitment and Selection' from ACAS (see Appendix).

Key points

- There are many sources of recruitment. The small business owner or manager needs to consider all of them – and their respective advantages and disadvantages – before deciding which will help him to recruit the right employees.
- Having sought professional advice, a job advertisement must be drawn up. Its contents – based on the job description and person specification – should be brief, specific and truthful. Its design must be eye-catching and interesting.
- A method of pre-screening – by application form, curriculum vitae, letter or telephone – has to be chosen to reduce a lengthy list of applicants to a shortlist of perhaps six to be interviewed. Pleasant, rejection letters should be promptly sent to failed applicants.
- To be successful, interviews ought to be carefully planned and well run. An interviewing method – one-to-one or panel – must be picked. A quiet office or room has to be found. Topics and questions should be prepared. Consideration needs to be given to the best way of opening, conducting and closing interviews.
- Following interviews, an offer of employment should be made to a suitable candidate. One or two candidates can be kept in reserve in case the offer is refused. On acceptance, a written statement of the main terms of employment may be issued and letters of rejection posted to the other candidates.

3

Training staff

Outline

All employees – from new recruits to long servers – need to be trained and assessed regularly to maintain high standards. This chapter examines:

- induction;
- identifying training needs;
- training methods;
- planning a training programme;
- evaluating training;
- staff assessment.

Induction

The process of installing a new employee should:

- educate the employee about all aspects of the job;
- give him the confidence to do the job well;
- ensure he fits in as part of the team;
- highlight potential problems so they can be dealt with promptly;
- be completed as quickly and as smoothly as possible.

Induction should commence as soon as the job offer has been accepted and any conditions (satisfactory references, medical etc.) have been met. If you have not done so already, send your new employee *all* background information about the job and your business (job description, staff handbook, company brochures, catalogues). If he is moving house to live closer to your business you could also compile a local information pack for him (street map, addresses and telephone numbers of banks, schools, health centres).

You should invite him to come in and attend an informal half- or full-day induction course with you before he starts work. During the day greet him personally and give him your undivided attention all the time. Chat about your business, discussing products/services, the market, customers, competition and your plans for the future. Then discuss the job, running through the job description explaining exactly what he must do and what is expected of him. Check to see he is fully aware of *all* terms and conditions, such as hours of work, pay, overtime, holidays etc. Also talk about the work environment. Make sure he knows your business's rules, regulations and procedures. For example, does he know what to do if he is ill, off sick, has a complaint or is to be disciplined?

Take the opportunity to show him around the premises. Indicate who works where so he knows how to find them. Point out where the rest room, toilet, medical facilities and canteen are (if appropriate).

You can introduce him to his new colleagues, giving him the opportunity to meet his direct superior, workmates, subordinates and other people he is likely to come into contact with on a daily basis. Let him see them at work so he will have a better idea of what they do and what difficulties they face. Perhaps he could have coffee or lunch with them.

At every stage ask whether he has any questions or problems. He may be too shy to mention them without prompting.

Tell him what he needs to bring in on his first day. This may include, for example, bank account details if payment is to be made direct to a bank account, his P45 (if he has had a previous job) and his national insurance number (see 'Pay and deductions').

Finally, be sure to indicate you are always available for help and advice whenever he needs it.

Before the new employee starts work you should:

- Remind your staff he is due to arrive. Ensure they will make him feel welcome. Assign a 'minder' (either his immediate superior or a close colleague) to look after him for the first day.
- If appropriate, check to see there is a desk and/or locker available for him. Make sure they are clean and tidy.
- Prepare a personnel records file. Exhibit 3.1 indicates the information that should be kept about the employee. You should also

---

PERSONNEL RECORD

Full name

Address

Telephone number

Date of birth

Tax code

National insurance number

Disabled person's registration number (if appropriate)

Next of kin (in case of emergency)

Education

Qualifications (school, college, university, professional)

Previous employers (names, addresses, dates, job titles)

Date when employment commenced

Job title

Pay (basic, sickness, maternity)

Training completed (dates, on the job, off the job)

Absence (dates, reasons, authorized/unauthorized)

Accidents (dates, descriptions, injuries)

Discipline (dates, reasons, actions)

Grievances (dates, reasons, actions)

Much of this information can be obtained from the employee's application form and the written statement which should also be kept on file (as should any employer/employee correspondence).

Exhibit 3.1 Details required for a personnel records file.

obtain and read the ACAS booklet 'Personnel Records' (see Appendix).

On the employee's first day, it is important that you:

- Meet him yourself before passing him on to his 'minder'.
- Check at lunchtime to see he is happy and there are no problems.

- Speak to him again at the end of the day to check whether everything is satisfactory.

During the first week you should try to see the new employee at least once a day to check developments, eliminate any problems and deal with worries. Talk to his direct superior regularly to see if he is working well. Try to spot any weaknesses or shortcomings at the earliest possible stage so they can be nipped in the bud.

After one month you should fully assess the employee's progress so far. Talk to the employee. Ask whether there are any problems, or anything he is worried about. Listen carefully for signs of external difficulties that may affect his work performance. For example, if he has moved to your area try to find out if his family are settling in and whether he has found it hard to find somewhere to live. Then discuss progress with his superior. Ask whether he has settled in. Does he get on with his workmates? Is he doing the job well? Does he work hard, turn up on time, and take care with his appearance?

Consider asking the immediate superior to complete a staff assessment form. This is simply a document divided into headings which will help you to assess the employee more easily (see 'Staff assessment'). If the employee's performance is satisfactory, consider issuing a written statement of the main terms of employment (if you have employed him on a trial basis).

If you are dissatisfied with the employee's performance to date you must decide whether or not it can be improved. What is the cause of the problem? For example, is it simply inexperience? This may be the employee's first job or perhaps he has not worked for some time. Do make allowances. Do not judge too harshly. You may be able simply to show him what he is doing wrong or provide training of some kind. If not, you must consider giving him his notice (see 'Giving notice').

Following this one month assessment, you must continue to assess the employee – and indeed every staff member – on a regular on-going basis. Performance may be satisfactory after one month but could deteriorate thereafter (when he's not on his 'best behaviour'). Be watchful.

For further information on induction, read the ACAS booklet 'Induction of New Employees'. Refer to the Appendix for the address of your local ACAS office.

Identifying training needs

Training is vital. It will:

- ensure staff have the necessary knowledge and skills to do their work well;
- prepare employees for future jobs when others leave;
- keep the workforce up to date with developments and technological changes;
- increase staff satisfaction – they may see training as a perk, a chance to learn something new or even as a welcome break in routine.

To achieve these aims, you must identify the training needs of your staff. These may be highlighted during:

- The selection process – did a weakness become apparent from the employee's application or during the interview?
- Induction – perhaps a new recruit is unsure of company policy in a particular area.
- Talks with employees – an individual may come to you with a query that indicates training is required.
- Discussions with superiors – an employee's superior may recognize a minor problem at an early stage before it becomes a major difficulty.
- Staff assessment – regular, formal checks on employees' progress could show up their limitations.

Training needs may also be identified by:

- Your future business plans – perhaps you intend to produce or sell a new product range which would indicate training is necessary.
- Anticipated staff changes – are you planning to transfer or promote an employee or expecting a retirement soon? Should you be training a replacement now?
- External developments – for example, new legislation is to be introduced which may affect your business.
- Technological changes – rapidly improving technology may mean regular training is needed to keep your staff on the ball.

Having decided that an employee (or employees) needs to be trained, you then have to consider the best way to do it. There are a number of methods available.

Training methods

You need to think carefully about particular training methods. Will your training needs best be met by:

- on the job training;
- off the job training;
- distance learning.

'On the job training'

This usually involves an employee watching an experienced superior or colleague doing a particular task or job. Following this, he will attempt to do the work himself under supervision. This trainer–trainee relationship will continue on a 'watching and doing' basis until the employee is capable of working well on his own.

Consider the advantages of on the job training:

- it is cheap, although bear in mind the 'cost' of taking a trainer away from other tasks;
- it is easy to satisfy needs, the trainer can go slower or faster to suit the employee;
- the employee will gain practical, 'hands on' experience.

This method of training has disadvantages though:

- you or your colleagues may not have sufficient knowledge or skills to teach staff, especially if training is designed to keep them informed of new developments or improved technology;
- your training equipment and facilities may be inadequate for the task;
- you or your colleagues may not have enough time to train staff personally;
- employees asked to train other employees may not have the necessary authority and responsibility to do the job well;
- employees taken off other duties may resent having to teach their colleagues.

'Off the job' training

Training does not have to take place under your supervision or on your own premises. There are many off the job courses run by reputable organizations such as the Department of Employment's Training Agency and the British Institute of Management. These may be held on the organization's own premises or in local schools, colleges or even hotels. Off the job training has many benefits:

- courses are run by fully experienced experts;
- up-to-date information, equipment and facilities are available;
- employees encounter fresh ideas and attitudes.

This type of training does have limitations though:

- courses are usually expensive, especially when you add on the cost of travel expenses, lunch allowances and lost production;
- employees are often taught theory rather than practice and it can be difficult to translate classroom theory into work practice;
- the courses available may not match your precise requirements;
- your business may suffer if key members of staff are away.

Distance learning

There are organizations – such as the Open College and Open University – which offer correspondence courses across a wide range of business topics. A package of books and audio or video tapes will usually be supplied. These will often be supported by television and radio programmes. For example, the Open College has programmes on Channel 4 in the afternoon, the Open University on BBC 1 and BBC 2 late at night and early in the morning. Tutors will normally be available by telephone for advice or by letter for marking and assessing work. Residential courses are sometimes available too.

The advantages of distance learning are:

- it is convenient – employees can study during evenings and weekends;
- employees can work at their own pace;
- the training is professional and expertly presented;
- new ideas and opinions may benefit a traditionally run business.

Think about the disadvantages as well:

- it may be costly, although not as expensive as some off the job training;
- courses may be irrelevant, with too much textbook theory and little practical use to your business;
- employees will need to be self-motivated to work during their free time;
- working alone means the employee will lose the benefits of immediate feedback from the trainer.

Planning a training programme

Deciding which training method to use is difficult. There are many factors to consider. Answering the following questions may help you to make the right choice.

What needs to be taught?

A new recruit, uncertain of your particular business methods, will simply require internal training. Teaching employees about new technology to be introduced may be best carried out externally. Detailed information about legislation that affects your business could be obtained through distance learning.

Who is most qualified to teach your staff?

If it is you, decide whether you have the time to do it properly. If a colleague could do the job better, does he command the required respect and have sufficient authority?

Where should staff be trained?

Consider whether you have the facilities and materials to train employees well. In addition, would internal training disrupt other employees at work?

How long will training last?

If training is going to be a lengthy process, would it be best for the business if the employee was trained in his own time via distance learning?

How much will training cost?

Can you afford to pay for off the job or distance learning courses? Will the expense be exceeded by the information gained and the overall benefits to your business?

These brief questions should serve to start you thinking about the pros and cons of each training method. Try to make a decision appropriate to your individual circumstances.

If you plan to train your staff personally, there are many organizations which may offer further, professional advice to ensure you do it well. Contact your local Chamber of Trade and Commerce, Training Agency area office, Small Firms Centre or the British Institute of Management (see Appendix). You could also get in touch with your trade association (the *Directory of British Associations* – listing the names, addresses and telephone numbers of around 6,500 trade and professional associations in the United Kingdom – is published by CBD Research Ltd and is available in most libraries).

These organizations will also provide information about off the job training courses. In particular, contact the Training Agency's local area office and the British Institute of Management. Both run a superlative range of courses themselves. For preliminary reading, ask the Training Agency for their booklets 'Your Guide to our Employment Training and Enterprise Programmes' and 'People, Performance and Profits' and ask the British Institute of Management for 'Development Programme for Managers'. You should also approach schools, colleges and polytechnics in your area. They often run Saturday, summer and evening courses which may be of interest.

For distance learning, write to the Open University for details of the courses they offer (see Appendix). Again, the Training Agency runs a variety of open learning programmes. Contact them and ask to see their *Open Learning Directory* (which lists more than 1,000 courses with full details) and *Spotlight*, the quarterly magazine about open learning.

Evaluating training

You must always evaluate staff training to ensure that it is of benefit to both an employee *and* your business. There are four ways you can do this:

- talk to your employee;
- talk to the trainer;
- talk to the employee's superior;
- watch the employee at work.

Talking to your employee

What does he think of his training? Is it useful? Is it too difficult or too easy? What does he think of the trainer? How could training be improved? Is more training required?

Your employee's views are obviously important but do take his comments with a hefty pinch of salt. For example, he may highly praise a training course he *enjoys* doing, but is it of any real use to him?

Talking to the trainer

What does the employee's trainer have to say? Is the employee benefiting from the course? Learning new information or skills? What progress is being made?

Talking to the employee's direct superior

Has the employee's work performance improved? Has he mastered a new task or learned a new skill? Has theory been converted into practice? Have production or sales figures increased as a result of training?

Watching the employee at work

Do *you* think your employee has gained from his training? If not, why not? What should you do to rectify the situation? Does he need more training? Perhaps a different kind of training?

Staff assessment

In a small business you will probably be working closely with all your employees. As such, you should be able quickly to recognize and develop an employee's strengths, rectify weaknesses and deal with any problems.

Nevertheless, it is worthwhile formally assessing staff on a regular basis. Conduct your first assessment – or 'appraisal' – interview with an employee after 3 months. (Remember, you will have already carried out an informal one-month review.) Re-assess every 6 months (or according to need depending on how closely you work with staff on a day-to-day basis).

Regular staff assessment is useful because it allows you to:

- spot and appraise an employee across the range of knowledge, skills and qualities required to do the job well;
- highlight, praise and promote strengths;
- spot and work together to resolve weaknesses;
- identify training needs, potential grievances, disciplinary problems and promotion prospects at an early stage;
- keep an employee on his toes;
- assess staff morale.

Prior to an interview, draw up a staff assessment form. This is simply a document listing the main areas for assessment. As you will probably want to use the same form for all employees you are advised to keep to general headings (see exhibit 3.2).

Speak informally to the employee about the interview and its purpose at least one week before it is due to be held. Allow him time to gather his thoughts. Give him a copy of the staff assessment form and explain you will discuss and complete this together during the interview. (If the employee's direct superior is to participate in the interview, let him have a copy of the form too.)

ASSESSMENT FORM

NAME _____
JOB TITLE _____
DATE OF ASSESSMENT _____
LENGTH OF EMPLOYMENT _____

Please tick and comment where appropriate:

	Unsatisfactory	Satisfactory	Very Good	Excellent

WORK PERFORMANCE
COMMENTS

WORK RELATIONS
COMMENTS

GENERAL CONDUCT
COMMENTS

PERSONAL APPEARANCE
COMMENTS

TIME-KEEPING
COMMENTS

ATTENDANCE
COMMENTS

Please summarize your assessment of the employee:
STRENGTHS

WEAKNESSES

RECOMMENDATIONS (Please recommend ways in which the employee's strengths may be developed and weaknesses eliminated. For example, is further training necessary?)

ASSESSED BY:
SIGNATURE: _____   SIGNATURE: _____

DATE: _____   DATE: _____

Exhibit 3.2 A basic staff assessment form.

65

You should then prepare for the interview by reading through the staff assessment form, job description, person specification and – if appropriate – any notes made following the employee's one-month review. Consider his work performance. Chat to his direct superior. Decide how you will interview him. It is usually sensible to do this on a one-to-one basis (although you may wish to include his direct superior in the discussion). Think about where you will hold the interview (see p. 39).

Commence the interview by helping the employee to relax (see p. 41). Explain the purpose of the interview again. Work through the assessment form together, discussing his performance under each heading. Ask him how he thinks he is doing. What are his strengths? Praise them. What are his weaknesses? Decide how they can be eliminated (for example, more training). Discuss any problems. Listen to any suggestions he makes (for example, he may feel a weakness can be attributed to a lack of information about the work he is expected to do and could suggest improved communication is needed).

Close the interview by completing the staff assessment form, summarizing the main points of the interview and agreeing on the targets that should be aimed for. Decide when you will meet again.

Afterwards, implement any measures which may help to rectify his weaknesses (for example, arrange for further on-the-job training). Continue to check his work performance on an informal basis (or ask his direct superior to do this on your behalf).

If you want to know more about the methods and techniques of interviewing employees, refer to the books listed under Further reading.

Key points

- Induction must begin as soon as the job offer has been accepted. Information should be sent to the recruit and an informal induction course arranged. On his first day at work, he ought to be personally greeted, looked after and carefully monitored. Close attention should be paid to him over the first week and month, at which stage an assessment can be made of his progress to date.
- Training needs to be carried out to make the most of employees. The small business owner or manager has to be constantly looking out for gaps in his employees' knowledge and skills.
- The advantages and disadvantages of on the job training, off the job training and distance learning must be studied. An appropriate training programme should then be set up to meet employees' needs. Training ought to be regularly evaluated and amended as and where necessary.
- Staff must be formally assessed at periodic intervals to develop strengths and rectify weaknesses. Working through an assessment form together at a relaxed interview is the best way of doing this.

4

Employing staff

Outline

Owners and managers of small businesses have to be aware of all the basic rules and regulations of employing staff so they will avoid infringing the law and falling out with their employees. This chapter investigates:

- contracts of employment;
- pay and deductions;
- statutory sick pay;
- maternity benefits;
- holidays and time off;
- avoiding discrimination;
- health and safety at work.

Contracts of employment

A contract of employment effectively exists when an employee starts work, thus indicating he accepts the terms and conditions offered. With the exception of contracts of apprenticeship, a contract does not need to be in writing to be valid. It can be based on verbal comments made during interviews or subsequent informal conversations (for example, on an induction course). It may also be based upon information given in adverts, a written job offer or staff handbooks.

Do be aware that a written statement of the main terms of the contract (see 'Accepting the job offer') is not in itself the contract. As the name implies, it is simply a summary of the *main* terms. Other terms may apply as well. For example, in the interview you may have promised that the employee could always take two weeks of his annual leave over the Christmas period. This may not have been noted in the written statement but is still part of the contract.

In addition, there are many statutory rights which are automatically included in a contract of employment whether it is made verbally, in writing or – as is most usual – a mixture of both. Although some are subject to certain exceptions and qualifying status (as detailed elsewhere in the text) the employee generally has the right:

- to a written statement of the main terms of the contract (see 'Accepting the job offer');
- to a minimum wage (see 'Pay and deductions');
- to itemized pay statements (see 'Pay and deductions');
- not to have deductions made from pay unless required by law (tax, national insurance), by contractual agreement or with his consent (see 'Pay and deductions');
- to sick pay (see 'Statutory sick pay');
- to various maternity benefits (see 'Maternity benefits');
- not to be discriminated against on the grounds of sex, race or marital status (see 'Avoiding discrimination');
- to the same pay as a member of the opposite sex if the work is the same or of similar value (see 'Avoiding discrimination');
- to a safe working environment (see 'Health and safety at work');
- to time off in certain circumstances, such as jury service, trade union duties (see 'Holidays and time off');
- to belong or not to belong to a trade union as he wishes (see 'Staff representation');
- to notice of termination of employment (see 'Giving notice');
- to redundancy pay (see 'Redundancy');
- to a written reason for dismissal (see 'Dismissing staff');
- not to be dismissed unfairly (see 'Dismissing staff').

Note that these are guidelines only. Refer to the appropriate sections as indicated above for further advice.

A contract of employment can usually only be changed with the employee's consent. Otherwise, you may be breaking the terms of the contract which could lead to a claim against you for constructive dismissal at an industrial tribunal (see 'Industrial tribunals'). Therefore, always obtain the employee's verbal agreement to a proposed change first and then follow this up with written confirmation which you should ask him to sign as proof of acceptance.

Pay and deductions

Paying staff is a complex, and sometimes confusing, topic. Basically, you need to know about the following:

- setting pay;
- pay schemes;
- methods of payments;
- itemized pay statements;
- making deductions;
- operating PAYE ('pay as you earn').

Setting pay

Your wage bill will invariably form a major part of your business overheads. Naturally, you will seek to keep this cost as low as you can by not offering high wages which bite into your profits, perhaps even making your business unviable. At the same time, offering low wages can be equally damaging. You will find it difficult to attract and retain good staff, perhaps having to settle for second-rate employees. In deciding how much to pay, you must therefore strike a careful balance between two extremes. There are several questions you should consider before reaching a decision.

What can I afford to pay?

How much can you pay without adversely affecting your business profitability or viability?

What are the legal requirements relating to pay?

Bear in mind wage agreements made during collective bargaining (p. 115), individual terms agreed and the Equal Pay Act (p. 89). Some industries also have wages councils which set minimum wages that must be adhered to. Your local jobcentre will advise you if this applies to your particular business.

What is the current state of the job market?

Think about the number of people looking for the type of job you are offering. Is there a shortage? For example, there is a diminishing number of school leavers looking for work. To attract quality youngsters you may have to offer better pay. What about skills? Job hunters with particular qualifications and experience in a specialized area can often demand higher wages too.

What level of pay will attract job seekers?

Find out the current rate for the job – study adverts in jobcentres, employment agencies and newspapers. Talk to jobcentre staff who are always a useful source of advice. Make sure the salary offered is competitive.

What level of pay will keep staff happy?

Bear in mind the salaries paid to your other employees. What will their reaction be if they think you are paying a new recruit too much? What will his reaction be if he thinks you are paying him too little in comparison to the other employees? Can you get the level right?

What other financial benefits are available?

Other factors are as important as pay in making staff happy (or unhappy). What else can you offer employees – job satisfaction, security, good social facilities, a pleasant work environment, fringe benefits? See 'Satisfying and motivating staff'.

Pay schemes

Most small businesses pay their staff on an hourly, weekly or monthly basis. Pay is usually directly linked to the number of hours worked regardless of the quality of an employee's performance or the quantity of goods produced and/or sold.

A 'time rate' has several advantages, including the following:

- it is simple to operate and administer;
- it is easy to calculate the wages due (hours worked multiplied by hourly rate);
- the total wage bill can be anticipated, aiding forecasting and budgeting;
- it is less expensive than some other payment schemes (see below).

Consider the disadvantages as well:

- there is no incentive to work hard or produce/sell more goods;
- lazy employees can hide behind more industrious colleagues;
- staff will sometimes need to be watched closely and chivvied along to maintain high standards.

Alternatively, you could consider introducing an incentive scheme. Two in particular may be especially relevant to the small business. 'Payment by results' links an individual's (or sometimes a group's) pay to the number of goods produced, sold etc. 'Profit-sharing' relates to all employees, with bonuses given if the business achieves certain targets (for example, annual sales turnover).

The benefits of payment by results are:

- it can act as an incentive, improving work rate and performance;
- business profits may proportionally increase if more goods are produced and sold;
- staff morale and team work may improve (in group incentive schemes).

The drawbacks of such an incentive scheme include:

- calculating and checking individual production or sales figures can be difficult and often time-consuming;
- rivalry between individual employees may lead to conflict and bitterness;
- quality of work may be sacrificed for quantity;
- it may be hard to calculate wage bills, thus making budgeting difficult.

Profit-sharing offers the following advantages:

- it can motivate staff to work harder;
- team work may improve;

- morale may be boosted;
- interest in the success of the business will increase.

Profit-sharing schemes have their disadvantages too:

- some employees may not contribute fully;
- it can be difficult to decide how much each employee gets – should an administrator get more than shop floor staff and if so, how much;
- staff will share in the business's profits and this could make the business unviable.

For further advice on pay schemes, contact ACAS (addresses and telephone numbers of regional offices are listed in the Appendix). Their free booklet 'Introduction to Payment Systems' is also worth reading.

Methods of payment

You can either pay your staff in cash, by cheque or by transferring their wages direct from your bank account into their bank or building society account.

Cash

Some employees – such as manual workers – are traditionally paid 'cash in hand'. Full-timers without bank accounts, some part-timers and temporary staff – such as students – can be paid in the same way. Consider this type of payment if requested by your employees. If not, choose one of the other methods. Collecting cash from the bank, checking and dividing it into separate pay packets is time-consuming. Carrying large sums of money from the bank to your business premises is also a security risk.

Cheque

Paying employees by cheque can reduce the administrative work-load and eliminate security problems. However, do bear in mind that some employees may not have bank accounts and others may find it difficult to pay your cheque into their account (especially if they are at work during their bank's opening hours). Employees may also have to wait up to four days until your cheque has been cleared before they can draw the money from their account (unless a prior agreement has been made with their bank manager). If you decide to pay your staff by cheque, consider arranging a facility whereby cheques can be cashed at a nearby branch. Give staff a longer lunch break in order that they can do this.

Bank-to-bank transfer

A third, popular alternative is to arrange for wages to be transferred from your bank account to your employees' accounts every pay day. This reduces administrative costs and eliminates the security risk too.

For further information about paying staff by cheque, or bank-to-bank transfer contact your local bank manager.

Itemized pay statements

By law, most employees who usually work for 16 hours or more each week (or between 8 and 16 hours per week for at least 5 years) are entitled to an itemized pay statement when they are paid.
   This statement must detail:

- the gross wage;
- the amount and purpose of any fixed deductions (for example, trade union subscriptions) *or* the total amount of fixed deductions if a standing statement has been issued (see below).
- the amount and purpose of any variable deductions (for example, income tax and national insurance);
- the net wage.

As indicated, you can issue one of two types of pay statement. You can either list the amount and purpose of every fixed deduction or – if you prefer – simply state the total amount without specifying individual amounts or purposes. If you choose the second method, you must provide the employee with a standing statement of fixed deductions. This will detail the amount, intervals and purposes of every fixed deduction. It must be re-issued annually or earlier if any changes occur.

Issuing a standing statement will save you the inconvenience of listing each fixed deduction on every pay statement. This is especially time-consuming if you have many employees.

For further details, obtain and read the booklets 'Itemized pay Statement' and 'The Law on the Payment of Wages and Deductions . . . ' available from the Department of Employment (the address and telephone number of your local office will be in your telephone directory).

Making deductions

By law, the only deductions you are normally entitled to make from an employee's wage packet are:

● tax;
● national insurance;
● other *agreed* deductions.

Tax

Under the PAYE – 'pay as you earn' – scheme you must deduct income tax from the employee's weekly or monthly pay if he earns over a certain amount. This amount will vary from individual to individual but will be based on his personal tax allowance (plus various adjustments according to his own circumstances). As examples, a single employee with just the personal allowance of £3,005 (1990–1 rate) would not pay tax until his income exceeded that amount. A married man with the personal allowance of £3,005 and claiming the married couple's allowance of £1,720 (1990–1 rates) could similarly earn up to £4,725 without being taxed. Tax deducted must be sent to the Inland Revenue.

National insurance

If an employee is over 16 but under state retirement age (60 for women, 65 for men) and earns over the lower earnings limit (that is, the threshold above which national insurance is paid – £46.00 per week in 1990–1), then both employer and employee must pay class 1 national insurance contributions on the employee's pay. So if you are planning to employ part-timers, keep their income below this level to avoid extra costs. National insurance operates on a sliding scale with employees normally contributing from 2 to 9 per cent of their income between £46.00 and £350.00 per week (upper earnings limit). Employers pay from 5 to 10.45 per cent (1990–1 figures). Rates may differ if you have set up your own pension scheme for employees (see 'Satisfying and motivating staff') who can thus opt out of the earnings-related part of the state retirement scheme (refer to your local Department of Social Security office for advice).

Deductions agreed in the contract of employment

Make certain these are notified and agreed in writing to avoid subsequent disagreements.

The only exceptions to this list of deductions are if you overpaid an employee on a previous pay day (although even in this instance you would be advised to notify him in writing of the anticipated deduction and obtain his agreement to it); if a court has instructed you to deduct money from his wages to satisfy a court judgment against him (he may have a fine or debt to pay and his creditor wants it settled in this way); or, finally, if you employ retail staff. In this case, you may make deductions for stock or cash shortages if – and only if – you:

- issue a written statement to the employee detailing the total loss;
- make a written demand for payment;
- deduct no more than 10 per cent of an employee's wage in any one packet. The balance should be staggered over subsequent pay days.

Note: if you own a retail business, make sure employees know about these deductions *before* they start work.

Operating PAYE

'Pay as you earn' can be divided into four separate stages.

First, notify your local tax office when you take on a new employee. A new recruit will give you a P45 (a leaving certificate from his last employer) if he has worked before. You complete this, keeping one half for yourself (detailing his PAYE code and national insurance number) and sending the other half to your tax office (thus telling them you have recruited a new member of staff). If the employee has not worked before, you obtain a P46 from the tax office beforehand, complete it in much the same way as a P45 and return it to the tax office. Following this, your local PAYE tax office (which may not be the same as your local tax office) will send you a PAYE code for the employee (if appropriate) plus a starter pack comprising instructions for operating PAYE plus tax and national insurance tables and forms required for its proper administration.

You then calculate and deduct tax and national insurance from the employee's pay. The PAYE code (a number and a letter) indicates the employee's total tax allowances (that is, the amount of pay that can be earned in that tax year which is not subject to income tax). Look up the PAYE code on the 'free pay tables' which will indicate how much of the employee's weekly or monthly wage is tax-free. Deduct this amount from the employee's total pay, leaving taxable pay (that is, pay subject to income tax). The 'taxable pay tables' will then show you how much tax should be paid on that amount. Similarly, national insurance contribution tables indicate how much national insurance should be paid according to income. Complete a Deductions Working Sheet (P11) each month.

Inform the employee and tax office of total income and deductions each tax year (6 April to 5 April). Fill in a summary sheet. From this, complete a P60 for the employee and a P35 for the Inland Revenue.

Tell your tax office when the employee leaves. Before departure, obtain a P45. Fill it in, stating the employee's total pay and tax deductions. Give one part to your tax office, the other two parts to the employee for his new employer.

For further help, talk to your local tax office or PAYE Enquiry Office. Look in your telephone directory under Inland Revenue for addresses and phone numbers.

The Inland Revenue also supply the following useful booklets: 'Your Tax Office' (IR52), 'Thinking of Taking Someone On?' (IR53), 'Employer's Guide to PAYE' and 'Employer's Guide to National Insurance Contributions'. Remember, a fully informative starter pack will also be provided.

The DSS can give you 'National Insurance for Employees'

(NI 40), National Insurance Tables (CF 391) and Social Security
Benefit Rates (NI 196).

Statutory Sick Pay

Subject to certain rules and procedures, most employees are entitled
to Statutory Sick Pay (SSP) from their employers for up to 28 weeks
of sickness. The state will normally re-imburse employers for SSP
paid.

The rules for obtaining SSP are that, on their first day of sickness,
employees must:

- be over 16 years of age and under state pension age (60 for
  women, 65 for men);
- have average earnings equal to or above the national insurance
  lower earnings limit (£46.00 per week in the tax year 1990–1) – if
  in doubt, 'average earnings' should be calculated by taking the
  previous eight weeks' earnings (up to the last pay day before the
  first day of sickness) and dividing by eight;
- already have started work for you;
- have a contract for at least 3 months (some temporary/seasonal
  workers may therefore be excluded);
- be within the European Economic Community (EEC);
- not be involved in strike action;
- not be in legal custody;
- not be eligible for statutory maternity pay (which is available from
  11 weeks before the week the baby is due – otherwise known as
  the 'expected week of confinement' or 'EWC' – and runs for a
  period of up to 18 weeks);
- not have claimed other state benefits (such as sickness, invalidity
  or severe disablement benefits, maternity benefits) less than 8
  weeks previously – if an employee has recently obtained these
  benefits the local DSS office will subsequently issue him with a
  'linking letter' stating the date from when SSP can be claimed;
- not have already had 28 weeks of SSP (the maximum entitlement)
  unless payment ended over 8 weeks ago (see p. 80);
- not have had a 'linked' spell of sickness lasting for 3 years that
  finished less than 8 weeks before (see p. 79).

Employees who fulfil *all* these rules (and note that this can therefore include such groups as married women paying reduced national insurance contributions and part-timers) may be entitled to SSP if they also then comply with all these rules and procedures.

The employee must be sick (that is, unable, as a result of illness or disability, to do his normal work) for four or more days. Only *complete* sickness days count towards SSP entitlement (if the employee comes into work from 9.00 am to 10.30 am and then goes home sick it will not count). Also, the four sickness days must be in a row. Known as a 'period of incapacity for work' or 'PIW' by the DSS, these four days can include holidays and days off such as Saturday and Sunday. They do not have to include working days. For example, an employee who normally works Monday to Friday and who was sick on Thursday, Friday, Saturday and Sunday would form a 'PIW' even though he would not normally have worked over the weekend.

SSP is only paid for 'qualifying days' (that is, those days when the employee usually works). In addition, SSP is not paid for the first three 'qualifying days' or – as they are better known – 'waiting days', but starts from the fourth. For example, the above employee may be sick from Thursday to Wednesday inclusive. Thursday, Friday and Monday would be 'waiting days'. If other rules and procedures were met, SSP would be paid for Tuesday and Wednesday.

PIWs separated by less than 8 weeks are known as 'linked PIWs' and count as one spell of sickness. The three waiting days rule will therefore not extend to the second PIW. For example, if the employee was again absent from work through illness from Thursday to Wednesday inclusive a month later, he would (subject to other rules being met) obtain SSP for Thursday, Friday, Monday, Tuesday and Wednesday.

The employee must comply with all your sickness rules and procedures. Typically, you might ask him to notify you promptly by telephone that he is sick and to complete a self-certification form (simply stating he is ill and the reasons why) for between 4 and 7 days' sickness. After this you could request a doctor's statement confirming that the employee is still ill.

If you have an employee who satisfies *each* rule and *every* procedure then you must pay SSP. There are two basic rates, depending on average earnings. Employees who earn between £46.00 and £124.99 per week must be paid £39.25 each week (or the appropriate, equivalent rate per qualifying day). Those earning £125.00 or more should be paid £52.50 (or the appropriate, equivalent rate). Note that these figures relate to the 1990–1 tax year and change every April.

You can, if you wish, pay your sick employees a higher level of pay (although the state will only re-imburse you for SSP levels). This may be worthwhile to maintain staff loyalty and morale (see 'Satisfying and motivating staff'). Alternatively, advise staff finding it hard to make ends meet on SSP that income support may be available from their local DSS Office (suggest they read leaflet SP1, 'Income Support').

You are only liable to pay SSP for up to 28 weeks (that is 28 × £39.25 or £52.50) in any one unlinked or linked PIW. Therefore, if an employee was sick without a break ('unlinked') for 28 weeks your liability would end at that point. If he was sick for 14 weeks, returned to work for less than 8 weeks and then became sick again for a further 14 weeks ('linked') your liabiity would cease at the end of those second 14 weeks.

If, unusually, your employee had a series of linked PIWs which lasted for 3 years without entitling him to the full 28 weeks of SSP, your liability would cease after 3 years. For example, if his first PIW started on 7 September 1988 and continued indefinitely in short 4-day spells linked by gaps of 8 weeks or less then your liability would end on 7 September 1991.

Do note that if your employee has a PIW that does not link with a previous PIW (that is, a gap of 8 weeks or more exists between PIWs), he may be eligible for up to 28 weeks further SSP. For example, an employee may have already had 28 weeks SSP up to 9 February 1990. If he fell ill again after 6 April 1990 (that is, 8 weeks later) he would become eligible for a further 28 weeks SSP.

Pay SSP in the same way and at the same time as you would pay normal wages. You must also deduct income tax and national insurance contributions (plus other agreed deductions such as trade union subscriptions) from SSP.

You can reclaim SSP (plus the national insurance contributions you paid on it) by deducting the total sum from the national insurance contributions sent to the Collector of Taxes every month (see 'Pay and deductions'). SSP may cost you time but it should not cost you any money.

If an employee is not entitled to SSP you must complete an 'exclusion form' (SSP1(E)), available from the DSS, on which you state the reasons why it will not be paid. Do this promptly, within 7 days after notification of sickness at the latest.

When the employee has come to the end of his entitlement (for example, he has already had a spell of 28 weeks SSP) he must be given form SSP1(T) – available from the DSS – which he then takes to the DSS. He may be eligible for state sickness benefit paid directly by the local DSS office.

An employee who is leaving and who has had a PIW in the previous 8 weeks, thus potentially affecting his next employer's liability to pay SSP, should be given a form SSP1(L) for his new employer.

If – for any reason – a sick employee cannot (or can no longer) obtain SSP you should remain sympathetic (see 'Dealing with problems') and refer them to the DSS for further advice. Other benefits may be available. Leaflets SP1 'Income Support', NI 16 'Sickness Benefit', NI 16A 'Invalidity Benefit' and NI 252 'Severe Disablement Allowance' will provide further information on such benefits.

To administer the complex and often confusing topic of SSP successfully, you should:

- Set sickness rules and procedures. When should staff tell you they are ill? How should they tell you? What proof do you require?
- Inform staff of your sickness rules in the written statement, during induction, in a staff handbook or on a noticeboard to which their attention must be drawn.
- Obtain relevant DSS forms: SC1 – self-certification forms; SSP1(E) – exclusion forms; SSP1(T) – transfer forms; SSP1(L) – leaving forms; SSP2 – record sheets.
- Maintain records: keep leavers' statements, linking letters plus record sheets (SSP2s) showing sickness dates, qualifying days, payments made, not made, reasons why they were or were not made. Be scrupulous; a DSS inspector may wish to check them from time to time.
- Read further information about SSP. NI 227 'Employer's Guide

to Statutory Sick Pay'; NI 244 'Statutory Sick Pay: Check Your Rights'; NI 196 'Social Security Benefit Rates'; and FB28 'Sick or Disabled', are all available from your local DSS Office.

- Talk to your local DSS office for advice on your particular circumstances. The information given above can be no more than a general outline. Individual situations *all* vary and need specific advice. A DSS officer may visit you on request.

Maternity benefits

There are several benefits to which pregnant employees may be entitled.

Paid time off for ante-natal care

An employee – regardless of hours worked or length of service – should be allowed reasonable paid time off to attend ante-natal clinics etc. if she:

- can provide proof of her pregnancy (although it may appear churlish to ask for this);
- has made an appointment;
- can supply evidence of the appointment (for example, an appointment card);
- has requested time off.

If these conditions are met, you should pay her the appropriate hourly rate during her time off.

Statutory Maternity Pay

You may need to pay Statutory Maternity Pay (SMP) for up to 18 weeks to an employee who has stopped work to have a baby. To be eligible for SMP, she must:

- be employed by you for 6 months (26 weeks) up to the 15th week before the week her baby is due (that is, up to the 26th week of her pregnancy);
- have average weekly earnings equal to or above the national insurance lower earnings limit (£46.00 in 1990–1). If in doubt,

the average can be calculated by taking the earnings of the 8 weeks up to the 15th week before the baby is due (that is, the 19th to 26th weeks of her pregnancy) and dividing by 8;

- stop work because of her pregnancy (SMP cannot be paid for any week during which an employee works);
- inform you in writing that she intends to stop work at least 3 weeks beforehand (you can, however, accept a shorter period of notification if you wish);
- supply you with form MAT B1 (a maternity certificate) which will state the week the baby is due (formally known as the 'expected week of confinement' or 'EWC').

If the employee is eligible for SMP, you will have to pay one of two rates. Employees who have worked a minimum of 16 hours per week for 2 years (or between 8 and 16 hours each week for 5 years) are entitled to 90 per cent of their average weekly earnings for 6 weeks followed by a flat, statutory weekly rate (£39.25 in 1990–1) for up to a further 12 weeks. Employees who have been employed by you for between 6 months (26 weeks) and 2 years are just entitled to the basic, weekly rate for up to 18 weeks. (You may, of course, wish to pay your employees a higher rate of maternity pay or for a longer period – see 'Satisfying and motivating staff'.)

An eligible employee does have some choice as to when she takes SMP. The maximum period of 18 weeks consists of a core period of 13 weeks which must commence 6 weeks before the week the baby is due as otherwise she may not be able to obtain her full 18 weeks entitlement because SMP cannot be paid for weeks during which she works. The remaining 5 weeks can be taken either all before or after (*or* some before and some after) the 13-week core period.

You should pay SMP at the same time and in the same way you pay wages. Deduct tax and national insurance if appropriate. You can reclaim SMP paid by subtracting the amount from the national insurance contributions you forward to the Collector of Taxes each month (see p. 77).

If the employee is not eligible for SMP, she may be entitled to either Maternity Allowance (£35.70 per week for up to 18 weeks in the 1990–1 tax year) or sickness benefit from the DSS. Refer her to your local office (unless, of course, you still wish to pay her maternity pay, see 'Satisfying and motivating staff').

Return to work after the baby is born

An employee is normally allowed to return to work up to 29 weeks after the birth of her baby if she:

- has worked for you for at least 16 hours per week for 2 years (or between 8 and 16 hours each week for 5 years);
- has informed you in writing at least 3 weeks before she leaves to have her baby that she intends to return to work;
- confirms the date of her return at least 3 weeks beforehand.

If these requirements are met she is entitled to be either re-instated in her old job or, if it is not reasonably practicable to do this, a suitable alternative job. However, there is an important exception to this entitlement. Employers who employ five or less employees do not have to take the employee back. Obviously, a small business is unlikely to be able to keep the job open for her or to offer suitable alternative employment as it could be detrimental for the business to do so.

Claim unfair dismissal

A dismissal because of an employee's pregnancy will normally be considered unfair unless:

- her pregnancy makes it impossible for her to do the job properly;
- it would contravene the law to have a pregnant employee doing that particular job.

Even in these circumstances, you should still seek to offer your employee suitable alternative employment to avoid a possible claim of unfair dismissal (see 'Dismissing staff') or sex discrimination (see 'Avoiding discrimination') at an industrial tribunal (see 'Industrial tribunals').

Maternity benefits are a complicated topic. If relevant to you, read the following publications which are available from the DSS: 'A Guide to Maternity Benefits' (NI 17A); 'Babies and Benefits' (FB8); and, in particular, 'Employers Guide to Statutory Maternity Pay' (NI 257). Contact your local DSS office if you require specific, individual advice.

Holidays and time off

An employee's entitlement to paid holidays (including public and bank holidays) must be detailed in the written statement of the main terms of employment (see p. 50). Every employee will expect a reasonable paid holiday entitlement according to his status. Operate a sliding scale starting at 18 days (plus public and bank holidays) for trainees and junior employees rising to perhaps 30 days for more senior staff. Reward performance and/or promotion with extra paid holiday, it acts as an incentive (see 'Satisfying and motivating staff').

In addition to holidays, some employees may be entitled to reasonable time off for a variety of other reasons. As previously detailed, a pregnant employee is allowed time off with pay to receive ante-natal care if she has made an appointment, asked for time off and can – on request – show you an appointment card and proof of pregnancy (see 'Maternity benefits').

Employees under notice of redundancy can take paid time off to look for work or to arrange training for future employment if they have worked for you for at least 16 hours per week for 2 years. (Alternatively, they must have worked for between 8 and 16 hours each week for 5 years.) For further information, see 'Redundancy' and also read 'Facing Redundancy – Time Off for Job Hunting or to Arrange Training', a free booklet available from your local Department of Employment (the address and telephone number will be in your telephone directory).

If you recognize a trade union for collective bargaining (see 'Staff representation') its members are allowed time off to carry out trade union duties if you have agreed to let them do this in working hours. It is up to you to decide. Time off will be with pay for officials and unpaid for non-officials. The ACAS booklet 'Time Off for Trade Union Duties and Activities' should be studied. For the address of your local ACAS office see the Appendix.

Although it is generally for you to decide whether trade union members are allowed to pursue union activities during working hours, you *must* give trade union safety officers paid time off to receive appropriate training. This is not only a legal requirement but in your own interests too – they may give you considerable help and advice on health and safety matters (see 'Health and safety at work').

Employees who perform public duties – local councillors, justices of the peace, local school governors, members of health and water authorities – are entitled to unpaid time off (see 'Dealing with problems').

Sometimes, an employee will be called for jury service. It is for you to decide whether you will pay him in these circumstances. Do remember that some court cases can last for weeks or months and that if you choose not to pay his wages he can claim an allowance (albeit limited) from the court.

You may also grant time off (paid or unpaid) if an employee asks for paternity leave or suffers a bereavement. In such situations, time off will be at your discretion. You must decide how much to offer.

Finally, you should note that an employee should only ever take *reasonable* time off. The definition of 'reasonable' is open to debate and will normally be the subject of discussion between you and the employee before time off is taken. It will depend largely on your type of business, the amount of time off requested and the effect of the employee's absence on your business. Try to reach an amicable compromise.

If paid time off is taken, the employee should be paid at the 'appropriate hourly rate'. Take his normal weekly pay and divide it by the number of hours usually worked to calculate the appropriate hourly rate.

Avoiding discrimination

In recent years, laws have been passed aimed at preventing unlawful discrimination against people on the grounds of their sex, marital status or race. Legislation also exists in relation to equal pay and the employment of registered disabled persons. To ensure you do not contravene the law, you need to be aware of the terms of the following acts.

The Sex Discrimination Act 1975

Under the terms of this act, unlawful discrimination exists if a person is treated less favourably because of their sex or marital status than another person of the opposite sex or marital status would be in a similar situation. This is known as 'direct discrimination'. Examples could include a woman who is refused employment because it is 'a man's job' or a married person who is not taken on as the employer wants 'a single person without family commitments'.

Some forms of unlawful discrimination can be less obvious. 'Indirect discrimination' exists when an employer sets a requirement which appears to apply equally to people of both sexes and marital status but which in practice tends to favour one group more than another. For example, a minimum height or weight requirement would favour men who are usually taller and heavier than women.

Unlawful discrimination is prohibited at all times. You must be careful not to discriminate – directly or indirectly – during the recruitment and selection process. Think carefully when drawing up a job description and person specification. Seek advice when drafting job adverts. Do not put questions on application forms – or ask them at interviews – that may be considered discriminatory. When you decide to make a job offer, a person's sex or marital status should not have influenced your decision. In addition, you must offer the same terms (hours, holidays) that you would have offered a person of the opposite sex or marital status.

During employment, the employee must be given the same opportunities on the same terms as a person of the opposite sex or marital status. He – or she – must be allowed to have equal access to training, transfer or promotion and to equally enjoy all facilities, services and benefits.

Dismissal for discriminatory reasons is unlawful as is the selection of employees for redundancy on the grounds of their sex or marital status (see 'Dismissing staff' and 'Redundancy' respectively).

This act applies to the following groups:

- Women *and* men – for example, if an employer refused to allow a man to put his child in the company crèche because it was 'only
- for female employees' use', the employer would be guilty of unlawful discrimination;
- part-time staff, regardless of hours;
- self-employed people;
- apprentices and trainees;
- pregnant women (see also 'Maternity benefits').

There are a number of exceptions to the act. It does not apply if:

- The employee works wholly or mainly outside Great Britain, although many other countries have similar laws.
- The job is in a private household and there is a good reason to employ a person of a particular sex. A recent industrial tribunal turned down a man's claim of unlawful discrimination against him by a private household who had refused to employ him as a nanny. The lady of the house regularly bathed with her child before passing him to the nanny to be dried. She claimed she could not employ a man for the job as she would be embarrassed if he saw her naked.
- There is a 'genuine occupational qualification', for example, if a job had to be held by a male or female to maintain decency or privacy – a changing room attendant – or if a job had to be taken by a man or woman for reasons of authenticity – an actor or a model.

The Equal Opportunities Commission is a public body established to promote equal opportunities between the sexes and to provide help and advice on the subject of discrimination (and how to avoid it). Contact addresses and telephone numbers are listed in the Appendix should you require assistance.

Useful booklets are also provided free of charge by the Equal Opportunities Commission (although do send a large stamped addressed envelope). They include: 'Equal Opportunities: A Guide for Employers', 'Guidelines for Equal Opportunities Employers', 'Sex Discrimination Decisions' and 'A Model Equal Opportunity Policy'. These are all well worth reading.

The Race Relations Act 1976

It is unlawful to discriminate against a person on the grounds of their race, colour or ethnic or national origins.

As previously indicated, discrimination can be 'direct', that is, where such a person is treated less favourably than a person of a different race, colour etc. would be in similar circumstances, or 'indirect', that is where a particular requirement favours one particular group over another.

As with the Sex Discrimination Act, you must not discriminate during recruitment (job adverts, screening, interviewing), when deciding who should be offered the job or when terms are offered. During employment, every employee must be given an equal chance to enjoy training, transfer, promotion, benefits and facilities on equal terms. Similarly, they must be treated fairly regarding dismissal or redundancy.

The main exceptions to this act are if the job is in a private household or there is a 'genuine occupational qualification' (for example, a model of a particular ethnic origin is required).

For further information contact the Commission for Racial Equality or the Race Relations Employment Advisory Service (addresses and telephone numbers are listed in the Appendix). Both provide free, nationwide guidance and advice on achieving racial equality.

The Equal Pay Act 1970

An employee is entitled to the same pay and terms of employment (hours of work, holidays) as another employee if the work they are doing for an employer is the same, 'broadly similar' (that is, the differences between the jobs are insignificant) or 'of equal value' (that is, the same, or a similar, amount of skill, effort and experience is required).

The act applies equally to all staff regardless of their type of job (manual, clerical, managerial), the business (shop, office, factory) or the hours worked (part-time, full-time). The only real exception is if the employer has set up a scheme whereby he pays his employees (male and female) more money after a number of years' service (see 'Satisfying and motivating staff').

For more details, contact your local jobcentre, ACAS or the Equal Opportunities Commission (addresses and telephone numbers are listed in the Appendix).

The employment of registered disabled persons

A business which employs twenty or more people must – by law – have at least 3 per cent of its workforce as registered disabled persons. The only real exception is if your trade is especially dangerous in which case you may be able to obtain an exemption certificate.

You may get information about employing registered disabled people from your local jobcentre, which can help you in many ways. Jobcentres maintain a register of disabled persons who are looking for work and will supply you with details of potentially suitable candidates. In addition, they can put you in touch with 'Disablement Resettlement Officers', who help people with particular health problems or disabilities find and keep jobs and who also issue exemption certificates, and the Disablement Advisory Service, which aims to encourage employers to take on more disabled persons. Both will provide you with useful help and advice.

There are also a number of schemes available if you are going to employ registered disabled people. Grants of £45 per week (1990 rate) may be given to an employer who employs a disabled person on a trial basis to see if he can do the job. An allowance of up to £6,000 (1990 limit) may be provided for employers who have to adapt premises or equipment in order to take on disabled staff.

Assistance can also be given to the employee (which may in turn benefit you). Special equipment can be lent to disabled persons who need it to do the job well. Financial help may be offered to those who cannot use public transport and need to seek an alternative method of travel. Money may also be provided for the visually handicapped who have to employ a part-time sighted reader to help them in their work.

If you contravene the Sex Discrimination Act, Race Relations Act, Equal Pay Act or the law on employing disabled persons, you could be taken to an industrial tribunal (see 'Industrial tribunals'). So, always be scrupulously fair. If in doubt, seek advice from one of the sources indicated.

Health and safety at work

You must look after the health, safety and welfare of your staff. It is your responsibility. A number of statutes have been passed to which you should adhere – The Factories Act 1961, The Offices, Shops and Railway Premises Act 1963 and – amalgamating and developing these two acts – The Health and Safety at Work Act 1974.

This last-named act covers all premises. To comply with it you must:

- Provide a safe work environment. For example, all floors, stairs and passages should be well constructed and free of dangerous obstructions or substances such as slippery grease or oil.
- Ensure comfortable work conditions – satisfactory heating, ventilation, lighting and clean catering, welfare and toilet facilities.
- Establish and follow safe work systems.
- Maintain safety standards on plant, machinery and equipment. For example, fence off dangerous machinery, check it regularly and repair when required.
- Keep noise, dirt and fumes to safe limits.
- Handle, store and transport goods and substances safely.
- Supply your employees with sufficient information, training, guidance and supervision to maintain health and safety (do this on an ongoing basis – employees do forget and become careless).
- Compile a health and safety written policy statement (if you have five or more employees) outlining your health and safety rules and procedures. This should be drawn up after consultation with trade union safety representatives (if appropriate), kept up to date and always be on display for staff to see.
- Allow trade union safety representatives paid time off to attend training on health and safety matters.
- Establish a safety committee to discuss and improve health and safety at work (if requested by the trade union).
- Supply – free of charge – protective clothing and equipment (if appropriate).
- Maintain adequate first aid facilities. Even the smallest business should keep a well-stocked first aid box, tell employees where it is, how equipment is used and ideally a trained first aider should be on the premises too – this is recommended if you employ fifty or more employees.
- Report injuries. *All* accidents should be noted in an accident book – date, time, location, description of injury, action taken, results. The local health and safety executive should be notified within 7 days of an accident if it results in absence from work for 3 or more days, immediate notification by telephone should be given for

serious injuries – loss of eyesight, limbs – followed by written notification.

- Under the Factories Act and the Offices, Shops and Railway Premises Act, all such businesses must register with either the local Health and Safety Executive (factories) or the local authority (offices and shops) if they are to employ staff.

If you run an industrial business (factory) you can obtain further, specific information appropriate to your individual circumstances from the health and safety inspectors from your local Health and Safety Executive. Addresses and telephone numbers will be in your local telephone directory.

If you operate another type of business (shop, office), get in touch with the health and safety inspectors in the Environmental Health Department of your local authority. Check your telephone directory for details.

Whatever business you have, do read further on this topic. The following, free leaflets can be obtained from the local Health and Safety Executive (HSE) offices: 'The Act Outlined – Health and Safety at Work Act 1974' (HSC2); 'Writing a Safety Policy Statement: advice to employers' (HSC6); 'First Aid Provisions in Small Workplaces: your questions answered' (IND(G)3(L)); and 'Short Guide to the Employer's Liability (Compulsory Insurance) Act 1969' (HSE4). There are, in addition, a wide selection of other leaflets available regarding particular trades and industries. Visit the HSE, have a chat and see what is available that is appropriate to your business.

Key points

- There is far more to a contract of employment than just a written statement of the main terms of employment. The small business owner or manager needs to be aware that it can also include terms based upon verbal comments made to an employee and written information given to him. In addition, every employee has a number of statutory rights that must be complied with.

- Paying staff is a complex issue which ought to be carefully thought about and fully understood. Special attention should be given to the amount to be paid and the method of payment. Issuing itemized pay statements and deducting tax and national insurance under the PAYE system will mean advice and guidance is required from the Inland Revenue and DSS.
- Statutory Sick Pay (SSP) may have to be paid to an employee who is ill for up to 28 weeks. Rules and procedures are so involved that only the DSS can supply advice which is relevant to particular circumstances.
- Pregnant employees may be entitled to paid time off for ante-natal care, Statutory Maternity Pay (SMP), to return to work after the birth and to claim unfair dismissal if sacked because of their pregnancy. Once again, this is a complicated area and guidance must be sought from the local DSS office.
- As well as expecting a fair holiday allowance, staff should also be allowed time off for various other reasons such as to carry out jury service or perform public duties. The amount of time taken ought to be reasonable, as agreed between employer and employee.
- Employers must not discriminate against people because of their sex, marital status or race. The Sex Discrimination Act, Race Relations Act and Equal Pay Act need to be read and adhered to at all times.
- It is the employer's responsibility to look after the health, safety and welfare of his staff. The Health and Safety at Work Act should be studied. Where necessary, further information can be obtained from the Health and Safety Executive or the Environmental Health Department of the local authority.

5

Controlling staff

Outline

From time to time, difficulties will develop between an employer and his employees. Many of these can be avoided, or quickly solved, if rules and procedures are well established. This chapter examines:

- making decisions;
- setting rules and procedures;
- disciplinary procedure;
- grievance procedure.

Making decisions

Decision-making can be extremely difficult, especially for the small businessman who has recently taken on staff for the first time.

Before making a decision, always ask yourself the following questions:

- What exactly is the decision I have to make?
- What options are available to me?
- What are the advantages and disadvantages of each option?
- What are the likely results of each option?
- What will be the benefits and drawbacks of those results?
- Do I have all the information necessary to make the right decision?
- Have I taken account of all the circumstances?
- Is my decision logical, fair and consistent?

Many decisions, so far as controlling staff is concerned, are relatively easy to reach if you set rules and procedures which must be adhered to. They provide a framework in which decisions can be made. For more information on decision-making consult the books listed under 'Further reading'.

Setting rules and procedures

Every employee needs – and wants – to know the following:

- A clear understanding of the job requirements.
- The standards of job performance that are considered satisfactory.
- The standards of conduct required.
- The rules that must be adhered to if job performance and conduct are to be satisfactorily maintained.
- The disciplinary procedure that may result if rules are broken (see p. 97).
- The grievance procedure that exists should the employee wish to complain (see p. 100).

Rules help to set standards of work performance and the boundaries of acceptable behaviour. Procedures help to deal with situations where rules have been broken and will also, hopefully, ensure that the rules will be adhered to in the future.

It is important that rules are fully stated in writing in either a staff handbook or on a noticeboard. They must be accessible to all employees and clearly understood. Make it your responsibility to ensure they are.

It is up to you to set your own rules. The following questions may start you thinking about the type of rules you might have:

- What should an employee do if he is going to be late for work (for example, should he telephone you)?
- What should he do when he is going to be off sick?
- Whom should he notify?
- How soon should you be informed?
- How should you be told (for example, by telephone or letter)?
- Should he provide a self-certificate for between 4 and 7 days' sickness (see 'Statutory Sick Pay')?
- Should he obtain a doctor's certificate after 7 days' sickness (see 'Statutory Sick Pay')?
- What should he do if he wants time off?
- Whom should he ask for permission?
- How much notice of time off should be given?
- When can holidays be taken (for example, not over the Christmas period)?

- Who has first choice of holiday weeks (for example, be careful to avoid all employees having the first two weeks in August which would leave you understaffed)?
- What health and safety rules should be set?
- Must your employees wear special clothes (for example, goggles, uniforms) or use special equipment?
- Should you have no smoking/drinking/eating areas?
- What work standards are expected?
- What about the use of business facilities?
- Can employees use the telephone for personal calls?
- Can work equipment be used for personal purposes out of hours?

When setting rules, you should also indicate to your employees what you consider to be unacceptable conduct. This can be divided into three categories:

- minor misconduct;
- serious misconduct;
- gross misconduct.

Minor misconduct

Such misconduct may possibly lead to a formal disciplinary procedure (see p. 97). Examples are: unexcused lateness; unexcused absence; unsuitable appearance; inappropriate clothing; excessive lunch or coffee breaks; failing to follow business procedures and practices.

Serious misconduct

This will lead to a disciplinary procedure, see p. 97. Examples are: persistent unauthorized lateness; persistent unauthorized absences; failing to report an accident; doing other work during business hours; inability to meet work standards; failing to observe safety rules and procedures.

Gross misconduct

This may *possibly* lead to instant dismissal, but see p. 121 for further details. Examples are: theft; abusive behaviour; offensive actions;

assault; gross negligence; refusal to complete a reasonable task; breach of confidentiality or confidence.

You should note that this is merely a guide, not an exhaustive list. In addition, bear in mind that each business may define cases of misconduct differently. For example, smoking at work may be termed 'minor misconduct' if it had been banned in an office because a majority of office employees found it unpleasant, but it could be 'serious misconduct' (or – in certain circumstances – even 'gross misconduct') if it had been forbidden on the factory floor for safety reasons.

Disciplinary procedure

Every business – large or small – must have an established disciplinary procedure it can turn to if rules are broken. Your disciplinary procedure should be:

- in writing;
- clearly understood;
- fair and reasonable;
- swiftly implemented.

In writing

In companies employing more than twenty people, by law, the disciplinary procedure should be detailed in the written statement of the main terms of employment (see p. 50) or in an accompanying handbook to which reference must be made.

Clearly understood

The procedure should be clearly understood by all employees and supervisors/managers who are responsible for administering it. Explain and discuss disciplinary rules and procedure during induction. Run through what the rules are, to whom they apply, who is responsible for enforcing them, what the results will be if they are broken and what disciplinary action may be taken. Personally ensure that no doubts or uncertainties exist.

Fair and reasonable

Your primary aim must be to rectify and improve work performance and behaviour, not simply to punish an employee. Your procedure should therefore always be fair and administered in a reasonable manner. Tell an employee about a complaint before taking any direct action. Give him a chance to explain and put his side of the story. Check all facts and look at every angle before reaching a decision. An employee should also be allowed to be accompanied by a colleague or trade union representative during the formal disciplinary procedure, be given every chance to improve and have the right to appeal.

Swiftly implemented

Attend to disciplinary matters promptly. If you hesitate uncertainly, you may lose face and, more importantly, control of your staff. They may think they can get away with breaking rules too.

In practice, your disciplinary procedure should follow five steps:

- informal oral discussions;
- a formal oral warning;
- a written warning;
- a final written warning;
- dismissal.

Informal oral discussions

Many, 'one-off' minor problems – arriving late for work, unsuitable dress or appearance or not following normal work procedures – can be dealt with informally (often by the employee's direct superior). Ask the employee why the problem occurred. He may perhaps not know what is expected of him or be unused to your ways. How can it be rectified (for example, by demonstration or training)? Tell him what standards you expect. Be lenient with new recruits, especially youngsters who may not have worked before or women returning to work after having children. Do not be too keen to implement a formal, disciplinary procedure when 'a quiet word in the ear' may suffice.

Formal oral warning

If minor misdemeanours continue, you must consider giving the employee a formal oral warning. Before you do this though, you should tell the employee the exact nature of your complaint (for example, continued lateness or carelessness). Listen to what he has to say. Hear his point of view. Does he have a good reason? Are you being fair and reasonable? Give him a formal, oral warning only if you are sure that you are – re-state the problem, outline the areas for improvement, what you expect him to do to rectify the difficulty and what will happen if he does not. Agree a time and date when you will meet again to review progress (remember, give him every chance to improve, so be generous when arranging a time). Make a note of the formal, oral warning on his records. If – at the time of review – he has improved, this note can be deleted from his file. Do not forget to congratulate the employee on his efforts too. Always seek to encourage and motivate an employee at every opportunity (see 'Satisfying and motivating staff').

Written warning

If the employee's performance has not improved, you should think about issuing a written warning. Alternatively, if the employee's misconduct is serious then an oral warning may be omitted and you can move straight to this stage. Once again, state the problem, listen carefully – and genuinely – to what he has to say. Make your decision and, if appropriate, tell him what standards you expect from him, how he can meet them and what will happen next if he does not. Set a date to review the matter. Issue a written warning to him and keep a copy of it on his file. If the matter is subsequently resolved, it can be removed from the record. Again – if the outcome is satisfactory, congratulate the employee.

Final written warning

For continual, unsatisfactory work performance or behaviour, decide whether you wish to issue a final written warning. As always, to be fair and reasonable you must tell him why you are unhappy with him and give him the opportunity to explain before telling him what you expect, how this can be achieved and when you will meet again to discuss progress. Issue a final written warning to him making it absolutely clear that dismissal (see 'Dismissing staff') will follow if changes are not made. Keep a copy on file. It can be removed if performance or conduct are subsequently acceptable.

Dismissal

If the employee's conduct or work performance does not improve you must consider dismissing him with notice (see 'Dismissing staff').

More information on this subject can be obtained from ACAS which also supplies an excellent code of practice which you should carefully read. It is called 'Disciplinary Practice and Procedures in Employment'.

Grievance procedure

Employees must always be given the opportunity to complain or to appeal against disciplinary action. You should therefore draw up a grievance (and appeal) procedure for your staff. As with a disciplinary procedure, this must be:

- in writing – detailed in the written statement (see p. 50) or in an accompanying staff handbook;
- clearly understood by all concerned – raise the issue during an employee's induction;
- fair and reasonable – employees are entitled to make complaints, have them listened to and acted on fairly;
- dealt with swiftly – if possible within 7 days otherwise morale may be affected and ill feeling arise.

A grievance procedure in a small business should be quite simple and consist of two stages:

- An informal discussion with the employee's direct superior.
- A formal complaint (or appeal) to the employer.

Informal discussion

An employee should usually raise any grievance (for example, about bonuses or holiday entitlement) or appeal (for example, against a formal oral warning) with his direct superior. Always encourage your staff to settle matters in such an informal manner.

Formal complaint

If the matter remains unresolved, the employee should then raise the issue with you. Encourage him to put his complaint or appeal in writing. On receipt of this, you should meet the employee (and – if he wishes – a colleague or trade union representative acting on his behalf) to discuss the difficulty sympathetically. Listen closely to what he has to say. Why has the problem occurred? Is it a real, genuine problem? Is there another, more serious grievance hiding behind it? Are other employees involved? If so, listen to their opinions. Check all the facts from all sides before reaching a decision. Inform relevant parties of your decision in writing.

Incidentally, in an appeal procedure, the employee should have the right to appeal to the person one stage above the person who disciplined him. In a small business this may not be possible (the 'direct superior' and 'employer' may be one and the same person – you!). Consider going to independent conciliation, mediation or arbitration if this is the case. ACAS can provide a list of people who can help.

Similarly, do not be afraid to seek external help and advice when trying to reach a fair, reasonable decision about an employee's grievance. There are a number of organizations listed in the Appendix: 'Sources of advice', which might offer a decisive and unbiased opinion.

You may find two ACAS publications of interest: 'Conciliation between Individuals and Employers' and 'The ACAS Role in Conciliation, Arbitration and Mediation'.

Key points

- The small business owner or manager may find it difficult to reach decisions involving his staff. Setting rules and procedures that must be adhered to can help to make the decision-making process easier.
- Disciplinary, grievance and appeal procedures ought to be set out in writing, be fully understood, fair and reasonable and be implemented as promptly as possible.
- Outside help and advice should be sought whenever a disciplinary, grievance or appeal issue cannot be satisfactorily resolved between an employer and an employee. ACAS can be approached if independent arbitration is required.

6

Dealing with staff

Outline

All employers want to get on well with their employees. This chapter shows them how. It discusses:

- communicating with staff;
- satisfying and motivating staff;
- staff representation;
- dealing with problems.

Communicating with staff

Communication must be a two-way process between an employer and his employees. You need to put across information such as job instructions, changes in terms and conditions, rules and procedures and business developments. At the same time you must be receptive to communications – and feedback – from your staff. Listen to their opinions, suggestions, worries and grievances (see 'Grievance procedure').

Good, two-way communications will:

- improve employer/employee relations;
- increase morale;
- scotch rumours and gossip;
- reduce misunderstandings and mistrust;
- settle staff problems quickly;
- ensure the business runs smoothly and efficiently.

Communication in a small business will usually take place via:

- face-to-face conversations;
- staff handbooks;
- noticeboards;

- wage packets;
- suggestion boxes.

Face-to-face conversations

You communicate with your employees every day during informal chats and formal discussions such as disciplinary, grievance and staff appraisal interviews (see 'Staff assessment'). Clearly, you put across all types of information in such situations and have the benefit of immediate feedback. Are face-to-face conversations on their own sufficient to maintain good, two-way communication though? For example, do you talk to all your employees regularly? If not, will some of them feel left out and resentful because they are not kept fully informed or receive information from other employees instead of you?

It may be beneficial to have regular staff meetings. Perhaps you could set aside 30 minutes or so each week or fortnight (according to needs) to discuss important topics and give your employees the opportunity to ask you questions and voice their opinions. This will help to foster a good team spirit.

Staff handbooks

Even the smallest business should have a staff handbook full of information about the business, its facilities, rules, procedures and general terms and conditions of employment. This need not be a lavishly produced, glossy booklet. It can simply be a series of photocopied pages attached together and regularly updated by adding and replacing pages as required. Every employee should be given a staff handbook on or before induction (see 'Induction'). A copy should also be kept in a staff rest room for easy reference.

ACAS produce an excellent, compact booklet called 'The Company Handbook'. It is worth reading.

Noticeboards

This can be a useful way of supplying general information of minor importance to your staff (and vice versa). If you use this method do ensure that the noticeboard is well located. Will it be seen by the right employees? Draft notices carefully so that they catch the eye (see 'Advertising vacancies' for some useful tips). Make sure that notices pinned on the noticeboard are up to date otherwise employees will assume there is never anything new and interesting to read and will stop looking at it. Consider putting a junior member of staff in charge of the noticeboard (they may welcome a little responsibility) to ensure old notices are removed and new ones are put up neatly.

Wage packets

A note or letter to an employee attached to an itemized pay statement (see p. 74) is a very easy way of communicating directly with him.

Suggestion box

Small businesses must always be receptive to the ideas of their employees. A suggestion box (or book) is one way of encouraging staff to forward their opinions.

It can be hard to decide how to communicate with your staff. Thinking about the following questions may help you to reach the right decision:

What is the message I want to put across?

The message will be the primary influence on choosing a way of communicating – for example, information about business rules and procedures should, by law, be put in writing.

Who is the message for?

For example, if it is for all your employees you may arrange a staff meeting.

How quickly do I want to communicate?

Obviously some methods – face-to-face conversations – are faster than others, such as notices which take time to write.

Is it a confidential message?

If so, consider taking the employee to one side for a quiet talk or putting a private note into his wage packet.

Is the news good or bad?

For example, would it be better to impart bad news about redundancy face to face rather than in a cold, impersonal note (see 'Redundancy')?

How much detail do I need to give?

In-depth information is usually best supplied in writing. It can be put across in a logical manner and read carefully. In a face-to-face conversation you could forget to mention important facts, you may not make yourself fully understood and the employee may not listen properly. As a result, he may not have all the necessary information.

Do I need to know the message has been received and understood?

If so, a face-to-face meeting gives you the opportunity of receiving immediate feedback from the employee.

Often, the best way of communicating is to mix both verbal and written methods together. A face-to-face conversation should be followed by a written communication repeating and confirming the main points. Vice versa, a written method – such as a staff handbook – should be followed up by an informal chat or formal interview to ensure that it has been read and fully understood.

Communication is worthy of a book in its own right and a number of excellent texts are recommended in the References. Also, ACAS produces a useful and interesting booklet 'Workplace Communications'.

Dealing with problems

From time to time, most employees have personal or work-related problems which may affect their work performance. In a small business, you will probably enjoy a close working relationship with all your staff. As such, you should be able to spot difficulties at an early stage. At the same time, employees should also feel they can approach you for help and advice.

Deal with staff problems on an informal, friendly basis. Take the employee away from his (usually busy and distracting) workplace. Choose a quiet, private room where you can talk without interruptions (see p. 39). Take pains to put him at ease (see p. 41). You need to create a frank and open atmosphere so you can get to the root cause of the problem (an initial, superficial problem could hide a deeper, more worrying one).

Encourage the employee to talk about the problem ('Tell me what the matter is . . . ', 'Go on . . . ', 'Tell me more . . . '), and then listen sympathetically. Avoid speaking too much, just say enough to nudge him in the right direction, and be supportive – nod and smile at the right moments.

Try to get him to work through his difficulty himself and reach his own decisions ('What do you think you should do?', 'What do you think the solution is?'). If it is a personal problem, avoid getting too involved. You need to maintain the slightly distant and respectful employer–employee relationship. You must ensure the employee does not become dependent on you, expecting you to solve all his personal difficulties and anxieties. Also, with a personal problem, avoid making decisions for him ('If I were you I'd . . . ', 'If you want my opinion, you should . . . '). You will then be blamed if the problem persists or worsens.

If specialist help is required on a personal matter, nudge the employee in the direction of more professional advice ('Have you thought about talking to the DSS, Citizens' Advice Bureau, a marriage guidance counsellor etc?').

Agree on a solution to the problem. If it is personal, the answer may be for the employee to approach a professional counsellor. If it is a work problem, you may mutually decide that more training is needed. Always set a time and date when you will meet again to review the problem and then keep an eye on the employee's work performance to see that it improves.

Your attention is drawn to the sections 'Disciplinary procedure' for dealing with persistent problems.

Satisfying and motivating staff

To retain good staff you must keep them happy and satisfied. You should also seek to motivate them to work harder and improve their performance which will – in turn – benefit your business.

A small business can keep its workforce satisfied in a number of ways. The following factors should be considered as those most likely to make employees happy (or unhappy).

Pay

Money is important to all of us. An employee will judge his value to your business according to the amount you pay him. It must be competitive – in line with what he could earn elsewhere in a similar job. Wage differentials between your employees should be fair and reasonable to avoid jealousy and resentment building up (see 'Pay and deductions').

Holidays

The number of days off each employee is entitled to may be a cause of dissatisfaction if an employee feels he is not being treated fairly. Operate a sliding scale starting at 18 days paid holiday per year rising up to a maximum of 30 days (see 'Holidays and time off').

The work environment

Think about your premises. Is the heating, ventilation and lighting satisfactory? Employees will be unhappy if they have to work in a hot, stuffy office. What about noise? Can your staff work in peace? Employees will find it difficult to concentrate if heavy machinery is in use nearby. Have you thought about the layout of your premises? Does each employee have his own space in which to work? Is there room to move about freely? Make sure your premises are safe too (see 'Health and safety at work'). Have you considered your business equipment? Is it modern, up to date and easy to use? What about the furniture? Can employees sit comfortably at their desks in chairs which will not cause backaches and pains?

Extra thought must be given to the work environment if you employ disabled people. For the blind or partially sighted, make certain that corridors and gangways are unobstructed. Employees with impaired eyesight will also find it helpful if written documents are enlarged through a photocopier and any signs and notices are clearly and boldly written.

Employees who are deaf or hard of hearing may benefit from the use of such equipment as flashing lights, vibration pagers, head-phones or amplifiers. Staff who have difficulty walking or who are confined to wheelchairs may appreciate the introduction of such aids as ramps with handrails at the appropriate height, wide doorways and clear gangways, non-skid floor surfaces plus signs, instructions, shelves, switches and handles at a convenient height as well as adapted toilet and washroom facilities.

Consider the use of equipment such as large pens, big staplers, rubber gloves for gripping, easy-to-use telephones, sealing machines, franking machines and anything else that can help make seemingly simple tasks for an able-bodied person a little easier to do for his disabled colleagues.

This list is by no means exhaustive – you can do much more – but it will serve to set you thinking. The best way of deciding how to satisfy a disabled person's needs is to put yourself in their position. For example, why not spend a day at work in a borrowed wheelchair?

Find out more about providing a good working environment by contacting your local Health and Safety Executive and, if you employ disabled staff, the Disablement Advisory Service. (The local jobcentre will put you in touch.) Remember that you may be entitled to financial assistance if you adapt premises or equipment for disabled employees (see p. 90).

Social facilities

Offer your staff an active social life to improve team spirit, harmony and happiness. Encourage works outings, Christmas visits to the theatre, office parties, sports and hobbies. Involve partners too.

Welfare facilities

Always think about your employees' welfare. Is there a quiet rest room where staff can relax during breaks? If you employ working mothers, is there any way they could bring their babies or children to work? As a small business you may not be able to set up a crêche on your own but could you get together with other employees nearby to start a scheme? If you are interested, contact the National Out of School Alliance which aims to promote childcare schemes and the National Council for Voluntary Organizations (see Appendix).

Subsidized food and drink

Many companies have subsidized canteens or restaurants for their staff. This may not be financially viable for a small business, but you could still consider introducing vending machines for hot drinks and snacks and offering luncheon vouchers too. Look up 'Vending machine manufacturers and suppliers' in your local Yellow Pages.

Cut-price goods

Most businesses allow their employees a discount on their goods and services ranging from a nominal 10 per cent upwards. Always offer your workforce generous discounts. It helps to increase staff loyalty.

Company cars

Larger organizations often give high-ranking employees the use of a company car. Although this will almost certainly be prohibitively expensive for the small business person, you could perhaps consider allowing an employee the use of a company delivery van out of work hours. (Note: Check to see that your insurance policy will be valid in these circumstances. Extend your cover if necessary.)

Travel expenses

Alternatively, you could think about offering your employees help with the cost of travelling to and from work (especially for those who live a long way from your business).

Loans

Some employers give their staff low cost or interest-free loans for various purposes (such as towards the cost of removal and relocation expenses). If you are contemplating this, discuss your plans with your bank manager and your solicitor (make sure it is a binding, legal agreement).

Sick pay schemes

If you have read the section of this book entitled 'Statutory Sick Pay', you will be aware that sick employees are likely to suffer a noticeable – and potentially serious – drop in income during an illness if they have to rely solely on Statutory Sick Pay (SSP). Such a situation may result in disgruntled and unhappy employees. Many businesses operate their own sick pay scheme based on their employees' length of service. For example, after one year, the sick employee may be entitled to full pay for the first 4 weeks of sickness followed by half pay for the next 4 weeks. After this, the employee should just be able to obtain basic SSP. If you do decide to pay your staff their full wages during a period of sickness you will normally be entitled to a refund equal to the SSP due to him (see 'Statutory Sick Pay' for further details).

Private health insurance

Some employers take out private health insurance for their employees through organizations such as BUPA. Many of your staff will feel happy and secure knowing that they will be well taken care of if they are ill (but be aware that some may object morally and their views should be considered). Prompt medical treatment for your staff will also have benefits for you – the employee will be back at work sooner, fit and ready to re-commence duties.

Contact an insurance broker, the British Insurance Brokers Association or the Insurance Brokers Registration Council (see Appendix) for further information. You coud also get in touch with your trade association as they may offer special discount package deals.

Permanent health insurance

Similarly, you can consider taking out this type of insurance policy to protect your employees in the event of sickness or accidents. Effectively, the insurer will pay the employees' wages during absences from work. Once again, this means security for employees and financial benefits for you as you will not have to pay wages out of your own pocket when employees are ill.

For more details, speak to your local insurance broker or contact the Insurance Brokers Registration Council or the British Insurance Brokers Association (see Appendix).

Pensions

Employers who provide some form of pension scheme for their employees will help to ensure that their workforce feels secure about its future. Pensions are a complicated, ever-changing topic. As such, you should seek advice from your local bank which may be able to arrange an appropriate scheme for you. Alternatively, contact the Society of Pension Consultants (see Appendix).

Early retirement

Linking a pension to early retirement at age 50 or 55 may be attractive to your employees. It can help the business too as it will increase the opportunities for younger employees to be transferred or promoted.

Incidentally, if you have employees about to retire you may like to put them in touch with the Pre-Retirement Association, Focus and/ or Future Perfect (see Appendix). These organizations provide useful information about various aspects of retirement. They also run retirement seminars which may be helpful.

Increased job involvement

Giving employees more control and responsibility over their day-to-day work can be beneficial. For example, perhaps they could be allowed to vary their approach to a task and/or become more involved in the setting of work targets.

All these factors can help to satisfy staff and keep them happy in their work. Consider the following ways of motivating them too:

Incentive schemes

As discussed, the introduction of payment by results or profit-sharing can motivate employees to work harder and sell/produce more goods (see 'Pay and deductions').

Increased holiday entitlement

Offering additional paid holiday for employees who reach targets or who are promoted may improve staff motivation (see 'Holidays and time off').

Training

Sometimes, training can be seen as a reward for hard work and progress (see 'Identifying training needs').

Promotion

The possibility of regular promotion will act as a motivating force to your staff.

Personal motivation

You can personally motivate staff by having a good attitude. Always be enthusiastic about work. Show interest in what they are doing. Lead by example. Set weekly, monthly or quarterly targets for your employees to aim for. These targets could include producing or selling a certain number of items or learning a new skill or task. Encourage staff to reach their targets. Acknowledge their progress. Congratulate them when they succeed. Sympathize and encourage them if they fail. Re-set individual targets within their capabilities.

When deciding how to satisfy and motivate staff, consider all the factors involved and the likely results of your actions (see 'Making decisions'). For example, offering a successful employee extra holiday entitlement may keep him happy and motivated but what will be the effect on other employees? Will they feel you have been unfair and, as a result, become jealous and resentful? Carefully weigh the pros *and* cons of your actions.

Staff representation

In a small business, your staff will often not be represented at all. You will simply deal with each employee on an individual basis, mindful at all times of the effects those dealings may have on your other employees. (For example, agreeing to a pay rise for one sales assistant may lead to dissatisfaction amongst other sales staff who think they should be paid more as well.)

However, you do need to have a broad, general knowledge of staff representation in case your workforce wishes to be represented in some way. Equally important, you also need to know where to obtain further, specialist advice on particular topics.

In a small business, staff representation is likely to take one of three forms: a works committee, staff association or trade union.

A *works committee* may consist of a number of employees (representing the workforce) and you (and/or your managerial/ supervisory representatives). Often developing from regular staff meetings (see 'Communicating with staff'), expect to meet regularly to discuss issues such as the work environment, health and safety and rules and procedures.

Works committees should be encouraged as a two-way exchange of information, ideas and opinions. To be truly effective, you must be seen to listen and act on your employees' constructive advice and suggestions. If you do not, their interest in a works committee will dwindle and, not surprisingly, morale will fall.

Take a look at the ACAS booklet 'Workplace Communications' if this topic is of specific interest to you.

In some organizations, *staff associations* are formed by employees and you may wish to encourage this type of staff representation. Your employees will be pleased that you are ready and willing to listen to them. As far as you are concerned, the existence of a staff association may simplify negotiations about terms and conditions of employment.

Trade unions exist to protect the interests of their members. In a small business, employees who are union members will be represented by an elected shop steward. If your employees wish to join a union you should immediately ask yourself why this is. Accept it as an opportunity to assess your relationship with your staff. Are you keeping them happy (see 'Satisfying and motivating staff')? Are you communicating well (see 'Communicating with staff')? Their desire to seek representation may indicate there is room for improvement in your relationship.

If a union (in practice, the shop steward) approaches you to bargain on behalf of your employees, you face three options. You can refuse and continue dealing with each employee individually, *or* agree to 'representation rights' (where you will not negotiate with the union fully but agree to the union representing an individual employee during grievance and disciplinary interviews), *or* agree to negotiate with the union (thus officially recognizing it). You must decide which option to choose. (Note that you are under no legal obligation to negotiate with the union.)

You should reach a decision by talking to your employees. If a large number are union members (or support the union) you may be unwise to refuse to negotiate with that union as you would then invariably face an unhappy, dissatisfied workforce. So – ask their opinions. Listen to what they say. What do they want you to do?

Should you decide to recognize a trade union (that is, by agreeing to negotiate), it will automatically acquire a number of statutory rights. Basically, it has the right to:

- be given certain information, for example about the business's recent trading performance, for the purpose of collective bargaining (see the ACAS code of practice 'Disclosure of Information to Trade Unions for Collective Bargaining Purposes');
- appoint a safety representative who is entitled to paid time off to receive training (see 'Health and safety at work');
- be informed about the sale of the business (see the Department of Employment booklet 'Employment Rights on the Transfer of an Undertaking');
- be consulted before staff are made redundant (see the Department of Employment booklet 'Procedures for Handling Redundancies').

Similarly, members of a recognized trade union have the right:

- to belong to a trade union if they so wish;
- to participate in trade union activities at an appropriate time, usually defined as outside working hours – including breaktimes – and during working hours if agreed with the employer (see 'Holidays and time off');
- to reasonable paid time off for trade union duties (if they are union officials);
- to reasonable unpaid time off to participate in union activities, such as distributing union pamphlets and collecting subscriptions;
- not to be discriminated against, for example, regarding training, promotion, dismissal or redundancy, because of trade union membership or activities.

Note that employees who do *not* wish to join a trade union cannot be forced to become members or be dismissed for refusing to join.

When you recognize a trade union you will need to agree jointly a set of rules and procedures for collective bargaining purposes. In discussion with union representatives you must decide the way in which meetings should be arranged and the subjects for discussion (that is, which terms and conditions are, or are not, subject to joint agreement). Decide who will conduct the negotiations – you and/or a representative, the shop steward and/or a full-time union official? Agree on what facilities will be made available for trade union use. For example, will officials be allowed access to a works telephone? Settle the way in which information should be passed on to the workforce and decide what will happen if agreement on any matter cannot be reached. Always try to secure a no-strike agreement with a union in case of difficulties – most unions and employees will agree as they will appreciate that strike action may bankrupt a small business – and refer to ACAS who will arbitrate. Agree to abide by their decision.

If you can keep your employees happy, communicate effectively with them and bargain fairly with a union (or other form of staff representation), you should avoid damaging disputes or industrial action. If you are concerned about this possibility, however, you should seek appropriate advice. ACAS always provides practical, down-to-earth help (see the Appendix for the address and telephone number of your nearest office). Many organizations also run courses and seminars on the topic of industrial relations. Contact two in particular: The British Institute of Management and the Open University (see Appendix).

Your attention is also drawn to the ACAS booklets 'This is ACAS', 'The ACAS Role in Conciliation, Arbitration and Mediation', 'Using ACAS in Industrial Disputes' and, particularly useful, 'Improving Industrial Relations – a Joint Responsibility'. You may further care to read the Department of Employment's 'The Employment Acts 1980 and 1982: an outline' and 'A Guide to the Trade Union Act 1984'. Finally, a number of full-length texts on this subject are listed under 'Further reading' and are highly recommended.

Key points

- Communication between a small business owner or manager and his staff ought to be a two-way process. He must tell them about changes and developments that may affect them as well as being willing to listen to and act upon their constructive comments and suggestions.
- There are many ways of keeping employees happy and satisfied. All should be considered, possible effects assessed and, if appropriate, developed or introduced accordingly.
- Staff could be represented at work on a works committee or by a staff association or trade union. All might be encouraged as a means of improving the employer–employee relationship. It is important, however, to bear in mind the consequences of agreeing to negotiate with a trade union. Also, rules and procedures for collective bargaining purposes must be jointly set and agreed upon.

7

Ending employment

Outline

Sadly, most employer–employee relationships eventually come to an end. It is important to know how to handle this promptly and efficiently, with minimum inconvenience to the employer and distress to the employee. This chapter looks at:

- giving notice;
- handling resignations;
- dismissing staff;
- redundancy;
- industrial tribunals.

Giving notice

Both an employer and employee generally have a right to receive a minimum period of notice of the termination of a contract. The period required should be set out in the written statement of the main terms of employment (see p. 50).

By law, there are certain minimum periods of notice that must be given according to the employee's length of service. Employees who work 16 hours per week or more (or who have been employed for between 8 and 16 hours each week for 5 years) will normally be entitled to one week's notice after they have completed one month's service. This period of notice remains until they have completed 2 years' service. At this stage, they must be given one extra week's notice for every completed year of work up to a maximum of 12 weeks' notice. Therefore, an employee with 2 years' service is entitled to 2 weeks' notice, 5 years' service equals 5 weeks' notice and so on. Note that employees who have worked for 12 years or more will still only be entitled to the maximum 12 weeks' notice.

In return, an employee who has completed one month's service must give his employer one week's notice. However, this period does not increase. Employees with one month's, 10, 12, or 25 years' service only need give one week's notice.

As stated, these are simply *minimum* statutory periods. Both sides can agree to longer periods of notice. For example, the provision of one month's notice each way is fairly typical, especially for employees who are paid on a monthly basis.

Naturally, it is up to you to decide what is appropriate in your particular circumstances. You may want an employee to give you a longer period of notice. If you have established good relations with him and he is willing to give you perhaps a month's notice, this may be invaluable in allowing you time to arrange for a replacement. Nevertheless, you should be aware that if the employee subsequently decides simply to walk out without giving you that agreed notice, there is often little you can do about it. In theory, you can sue him through the county court but in practice this would probably be a pointless, time-consuming exercise. (Staying on good terms is probably your best defence against this happening – see 'Satisfying and motivating staff' and 'Handling resignations'.)

Think about the positive and negative aspects of offering an employee a longer period of notice than is legally necessary. It may make him feel more secure in his job thus improving morale, but what happens if you want to dismiss him? You certainly do not want a disgruntled employee on your premises for the next month causing problems. In practice, he will invariably accept payment in lieu of notice but even so, this will still cost you more money than is really necessary. Think carefully when reaching a decision about periods of notice.

Unless otherwise specified in the contract of employment, notice can usually be given on any day and need not be in writing. The period of notice runs from the following day. For example, if a week's notice is given on a Wednesday, the period of notice commences on the Thursday and ends on the following Wednesday. Normal pay should be given during the period of notice. Where employees are being dismissed, most are entitled to a written statement of the reason(s) for dismissal (see p. 125).

There are some important exceptions to these rights which you should be aware of. Either the employer or employee can terminate the contract without notice if the behaviour of the other party warrants it. For example, the employer may be entitled to dismiss an employee immediately, without notice or accrued holiday pay, for 'gross misconduct' – such as gross insubordination or neglect – (see p. 96). In addition, either party may waive its right to notice, if it so wishes. In some circumstances, both sides may agree it would be best if the employee left immediately.

The Department of Employment supply a free booklet entitled 'Rights to Notice and Reasons for Dismissal' which provides further useful information. Contact your local Department of Employment for a copy.

Handling resignations

In any business, from time to time, an employee will resign. Always interview an employee before he leaves: such an 'exit' interview has many uses. It will enable you to find out his reasons for leaving (as he no longer intends to work for you, he should not be afraid to tell the truth). It can highlight faults in your recruitment and management of staff and you can then rectify these, which may help to reduce staff turnover in the future. A face-to-face interview may give you the opportunity to persuade your employee to change his mind and stay. Such interviews can also improve your caring business image.

Many businesses simply ask employees to complete a form stating their reasons for leaving. However, some employees will always be reluctant to put their true reasons in writing especially, as is likely, if they might be seen as criticisms of the business. Comments made will therefore often be bland and, as such, of little use. An interview is always preferable. If handled well, you should be able to discover the real reasons for the resignation.

Prepare for the interview by deciding who will interview the employee. If there is friction between you and the employee, for example, it may be sensible for a colleague to conduct the interview. Study the employee's work record: read through staff assessment forms, talk to his direct superior etc. Decide where the interview will be held. Make sure you choose a quiet room where you will not be disturbed (see p. 39). Plan the interview out (see p. 40).

Open the interview by putting the employee at ease (see p. 41).
Tell him you are sorry he is leaving. Explain why you have arranged
the interview. Once he is relaxed, move on to ask questions such as
'What do you plan to do?', 'When do you want to leave?' (see
'Giving notice') and 'Tell me why you're leaving'. Think about the
way you phrase questions (see p. 43) and adhere to the simple
interviewing tips on p. 44. If you wish, try to persuade him to
withdraw his resignation. If not, end the interview by thanking him
for coming to see you and wishing him well for the future.

After the interview assess his reasons for leaving. Do they highlight faults in the way you recruit or manage staff? For example, do
you think you employed an under-qualified person, who simply
could not cope, just to fill the vacancy? Do you need to revise your
approach to recruitment or management? Do you perhaps need to
spend more time thinking about the type of people you should be
recruiting? Check staff morale has not been affected by the employee's resignation (see 'Communicating with staff' and 'Satisfying
and motivating staff').

For further information on handling resignations read the excellent ACAS booklet entitled 'Labour Turnover'.

Dismissing staff

A dismissal usually takes place when an employer terminates an
employee's contract either with or without notice (although it can
also occur when a fixed term contract expires and is not renewed and
when an employee terminates a contract either with or without
notice because you have broken one of the major terms of that
contract and claims 'constructive dismissal' – see p. 124.

Dismissing staff can be an extremely hazardous affair. You need
to know the differences between a 'fair dismissal' and an 'unfair
dismissal'. If an employee is unfairly dismissed he may appeal to an
industrial tribunal for re-instatement in the same job and/or financial
compensation. This may also create considerable adverse publicity
for your business and unrest amongst your other employees who
will be concerned for their own future.

Fair dismissal

To be a fair dismissal, you must have 'sufficient reason' *and* have 'acted reasonably' at all times. You may be entitled to dismiss an employee on the following grounds:

- Incapability. Does he lack the necessary skills, aptitudes, qualifications or good health to do the job properly?
- Misconduct. Continual minor or serious cases of misconduct may lead to dismissal as could gross misconduct – fighting or stealing – which may sometimes warrant immediate or 'summary' dismissal without notice or accrued holiday pay.
- Legal reasons barring the employee from doing the job. For example, if a van driver was banned from driving for 3 years by a court then his continued employment as a driver would be a breach of the law.
- Redundancy. In this case the job simply ceases to exist, for any number of reasons. See 'Redundancy' for more details.
- 'Other substantial reasons'. An example might be if an employee's partner started a business in competition with you which was likely to be successful because of confidential information about your business or products supplied by your employee.

These grounds could all contain the 'sufficient reason' you require to fairly dismiss an employee. Nevertheless, you must also 'act reasonably'. If the employee is, in your opinion, incapable of doing the job you should not simply sack him immediately; that would be unfair. You would not have 'acted reasonably'. Talk to him. Ask him why is his work poor? Does he know what is expected of him? Has he been shown what to do? Has he had sufficient training? Identify the root cause of the problem. For example, the nature of the job may have changed as a result of computerization and, as the saying goes, 'you can't teach an old dog new tricks'. Alternatively, perhaps the employee has just been promoted and has not settled yet. What is the solution? Does he need more information, training or time? To be fair, you *must* give him every chance to prove he is capable.

An employee who has been off sick for a lengthy period can, perhaps surprisingly, be dismissed on the grounds of incapability if, of course, you 'act reasonably'. Contact the employee to see if he knows when or if he will be returning to work. You must be sympathetic – this is a polite request for information not a demand to get better! Could he perhaps come back on a part-time basis? Are you in a position to offer him a different, less strenuous job (or remove the more arduous parts of his present job)? If he genuinely does not know when he can return, you could ask for written permission to approach his doctor. If – *and only if* – it is given, you may then write to the doctor (making sure you enclose your employee's letter of consent) explaining the nature of the job and asking if the doctor can indicate when the employee may be able to re-commence work. If the employee will not permit you to approach his doctor or, alternatively, the doctor does not reply, consider arranging for a private medical examination. The key points to dismissing staff because of ill health are to obtain a medical report and to give your employee time to regain his health – you cannot hurry an illness!

An employee who is regularly absent from work for short periods can also be dismissed as long as you act in a reasonable manner. Check your records to see how often he is off sick. Bearing in mind the pressures of his particular job, is he absent more than your other employees? Talk to the employee. Why is he absent so often? Is he generally run down or over-stressed? Does he need a holiday? Alternatively, are his absences unrelated to illness? If so, consider implementing your disciplinary procedure to rectify the matter or, if not, to dismiss him.

For misconduct, you should again adhere to the disciplinary procedure you have established. Minor cases – unsuitable appearance, lengthy lunch breaks – should be dealt with informally at first followed by a formal oral warning. More serious cases, such as repeated minor misdemeanours, should result in written warnings. Cases of gross misconduct – refusal to obey reasonable instructions, gross negligence – may sometimes warrant immediate ('summary') dismissal without notice or accrued holiday pay but do be careful. There is usually an opportunity to give at least one warning. Does the employee deserve a second chance?

For dismissal because of legal reasons that stop the employee doing the job, consider whether you can offer him suitable alternative employment. In a small business that may not be possible but you should certainly try to accommodate him elsewhere if you can.

In a redundancy situation you should, to be fair, consider all the following questions carefully. Is there an alternative? Could you eliminate overtime, transfer staff or ask for voluntary redundancies or early retirement? If not, is your selection method fair? Can you give plenty of warning and help redundant employees to find other work?

For a 'substantial reason' to be fair and for you to have acted reasonably, ask yourself the following questions (which could equally apply to other reasons too):

- Do I truly have a good, fair reason to dismiss this employee?
- Have I considered all the facts carefully and fairly?
- Have I taken account of all the circumstances?
- Have I considered all the alternatives?
- Have I followed a fair and proper procedure?
- Would a 'reasonable employer' dismiss this employee?

If the answer to these questions is 'yes' it would indicate that this is a 'fair dismissal'.

Unfair dismissal

An 'unfair dismissal' may occur if you do not have fair reason and/or have not acted reasonably as previously indicated. You must also be especially wary of an employee who resigns (see p. 120). If he is leaving because you broke one of the main terms of his contract, he may claim 'constructive dismissal' (that is, your behaviour was such that you effectively forced him to resign). In such cases, you may have to face an unfair dismissal claim at an industrial tribunal. Examples of behaviour that may result in constructive dismissal would include reducing pay, changing hours of work, failing to provide a safe work environment, unjustifiable warnings and making him do work outside his contract. Avoid potential problems by adhering closely to the contract of employment.

Employees who meet all the following requirements may be eligible to bring a claim of unfair dismissal against you. They must

- have been employed for at least 16 hours per week for 2 years *or* between 8 and 16 hours each week for 5 years;

- be below your business's normal retirement age or – if this is not appropriate – the state pension age (60 for women, 65 for men);
- work in Great Britain.

Employees who do not meet these requirements cannot usually claim unfair dismissal but do note that all employees dismissed on the grounds of sex, marital status, race, pregnancy or trade union membership or activities may be able to take you to an industrial tribunal claiming unlawful discrimination (see 'Avoiding discrimination' and 'Industrial tribunals'). Find out more about unfair dismissal by reading the Department of Employment booklet 'Unfairly Dismissed?'.

If you decide to dismiss an employee – and remember it should be a last resort – follow these steps:

- Seek advice if you are in any doubt at all whether you are acting fairly or not (see your solicitor).
- Meet the employee to explain your reasons for the dismissal (try to part on amicable terms).
- Give the employee the appropriate notice (according to his contract of employment or statutory requirements) or payment (including accrued holiday pay) in lieu of notice (it may be better if he leaves immediately – you do not want a disgruntled employee on the premises).
- Forward his pay, P45 and, if appropriate, an SSP1(L) (see 'Statutory Sick Pay').
- If requested by an employee who has been with you for 6 months or more, you must supply a written statement explaining the reason(s) for his dismissal. This request can be made orally or in writing. You must comply within 14 days.

The Department of Employment booklet 'Rights to Notice and Reasons for Dismissal' will provide further information.

Redundancy

Redundancy occurs when a job – or jobs – cease to exist. Typically, this could be because an employer stops trading as a result of a slump in the industry or he no longer needs a particular job to be done.

If you anticipate a redundancy situation, you must ensure that you fulfil your legal and – of equal importance – your moral obligations. Redundancy, especially for long-serving employees, can be very traumatic. You must handle these difficult circumstances well. Adhere to the following steps:

- Decide if any alternative exists.
- Select staff fairly and objectively.
- Give lengthy periods of notice.
- Consult with a trade union (if appropriate).
- Notify the Department of Employment (if appropriate).
- Allow staff paid time off for job hunting or to arrange training.
- Assist staff in finding new work.
- Make redundancy payments to those eligible.
- Claim a rebate on redundancy payments.

Considering alternatives

Have you considered all the options? Could you offer an employee suitable alternative employment elsewhere in the business? Can you transfer him to another department? What about retirement? Do you have any employees over the state retirement age whom you could ask to retire? Do you have any employees who may welcome early retirement? What about voluntary redundancies? Employees receiving generous redundancy payments (see below) may see it as an opportunity to start a new life.

Think about the choices available to you in your particular situation. Redundancy should be the last resort. Talk through your options with an experienced, independent person. The Department of Employment's Small Firms Service (see Appendix) offers all small businesses a confidential counselling service with an experienced business person who may have been in a similar situation. The first three consultations are free. Dial 100 and ask the operator for 'Freefone Enterprise'. You will be connected – free of charge – with your local Small Firms Centre.

Selecting staff

Your selection process for redundancies must be fair to avoid claims of unfair dismissal. Be seen to be fair. 'First in, Last out' is frequently used. If possible, agree objective selection criteria with employee representatives.

Giving notice

Always try to give employees selected for redundancy as long as possible to find another job. It may be especially difficult for older employees in their fifties to find new work.

Consulting the union

Discuss your plans with the trade union. Tell them why staff are being made redundant, how many, whom you have selected and on what basis selection has been made. By law, if you are making ten or more employees redundant, the trade union should be notified at least 30 days before the first redundancy. In practice, you should tell them as soon as possible and be as open as you can over the issues.

Telling the Department of Employment

If ten or more staff are to be made redundant you must also contact the Department of Employment at least 30 days beforehand. You should pass on the same information as was given to trade unions (why, how many, who etc.).

Helping with job hunting

By law, many employees are entitled to reasonable paid time off to look for new work or to make arrangements to be trained for future employment (see 'Holidays and time off'). It would be generous to allow all employees under notice of redundancy reasonable time off whether they are eligible or not. Give them every chance to find other jobs. Tell the local jobcentre and other local employers that the employees are available for work. You may also be able to help in other ways too, by letting employees use your facilities and equipment in their job hunting. For example, secretarial staff could type up letters and curricula vitae for them.

Making redundancy payments

Most employees with at least 2 years' service (excluding service before the age of 18) who work 16 hours each week (or between 8 and 16 hours per week for 5 years) in Great Britain and who are under 65 years of age (unless the firm has a normal retirement age below 65) may claim a redundancy payment from their employer if dismissed because of redundancy. The amount due depends on the employee's age, weekly pay (up to a limit of £184 for 1990–1) and length of service (up to a maximum of 20 years). For every completed year between the ages of 18 and 21, the employee will be entitled to half a week's pay rising to one week's pay per completed year between the ages of 22 and 40. Employees aged between 41 and 65 receive one and a half week's pay per completed year of work. Note that redundancy payments are reduced for employees within one year of the state retirement age by a twelfth for every month they are over the age of 59 or 64.

Incidentally, if the employer has financial problems, it may be able to arrange for the Department of Employment to pay the employee from a state 'Redundancy Fund'. (This will have to be repaid in due course.) Contact your local office to find out more.

The Department of Employment provides three very useful booklets on redundancy: 'Procedure for Handling Redundancies', 'Facing Redundancy: Time Off for Job Hunting or to Arrange Training' and 'Redundancy Payments'. ACAS can supply 'Redundancy Handling'. You should read them all carefully.

Industrial tribunals

Industrial tribunals are independent judicial bodies set up to provide a prompt and inexpensive way of settling most employment disputes. They are administered by the Central Office of the Industrial Tribunals. A London Central Office is responsible for England and Wales and a Glasgow Central Office covers Scotland. In England and Wales there are eleven Regional Offices and a

number of smaller Offices of the Industrial Tribunals. Scotland has
a similar network but without Regional Offices. Their Offices of the
Industrial Tribunals are located in Edinburgh, Dundee, Glasgow
and Aberdeen. Altogether, the United Kingdom has an adequate
number of permanent centres to hear cases, although additional
premises are sometimes hired if necessary.

An industrial tribunal consists of a chairperson plus two
members. The legally qualified chairperson is appointed by the
Lord Chancellor in England and Wales and the Lord President in
Scotland. He will normally be a solicitor or barrister of at least 7
years' standing. The members are appointed by the Secretary of
State for Employment. Their names are taken from two lists, one of
which is drawn up after consultation with employers' organizations
(for example, The National Chamber of Trade and the National
Federation of the Self Employed and Small Businesses), the other
after discussions with employees' organizations (such as the Trades
Union Congress and the Council of Managerial and Professional
Staffs). Typically, the two members would be a personnel officer
and a trade union representative without legal qualifications but
fully experienced in industrial relations. Whoever they are, they will
be trained, impartial and will reach an independent decision based
on the facts.

A tribunal will normally deal with complaints, disputes and
claims relating to many (but not all) of an employee's statutory
rights. The following will give you an idea of the type of issues it will
look at. Subject to various qualifying conditions, as previously
indicated in the appropriate sections, an employee is generally
entitled:

- to a written statement of the main terms of employment;
- to an itemized pay statement;
- not to have unauthorized deductions made from pay;
- to equal pay and terms;
- to paid time off for ante-natal care;
- to maternity pay;
- to return to work after maternity leave;
- not to be discriminated against because of sex, marital status,
  colour, race, nationality, origins, trade union membership or
  activities;

- to time off for public duties;
- to paid time off for trade union duties;
- to time off for trade union activities;
- to receive redundancy payments;
- to paid time off, if made redundant, to look for work or arrange training;
- not to be unfairly dismissed;
- to a written statement of the reason(s) for dismissal.

You should note, however, that an employee may only be entitled to these rights *if* he meets certain conditions.

The vast majority of cases brought to an industrial tribunal – around 75 per cent – concern complaints of unfair dismissal (see p. 124). Matters regarding redundancy payments, equal pay, race relations and sex discrimination form the majority of the remainder of cases.

The procedure relating to industrial tribunals is as follows. An applicant (that is, the person bringing the case) completes a form IT1 (available from his local jobcentre or employment office), detailing his name and address, the respondent's name and address (that is, the person or business defending the case) and information about his complaint or claim. This must be sent to the Secretary of the Tribunals at the appropriate Central Office, usually within 3 months of the alleged offence.

If the applicant meets any qualifying conditions (for example, length of service in the case of some unfair dismissal claims) and the matter is within the tribunal's jurisdiction, the application will be registered and details forwarded to the appropriate local office. The respondent is also sent a copy of the application along with a form (known as 'a notice of appearance') asking if he intends to contest the case and, if so, on what grounds. This must be completed and returned within 14 days of receipt.

Both statements – if, as is likely, the respondent intends to defend – are usually then given to a conciliation officer of ACAS who will endeavour to settle the dispute without recourse to a full hearing. In 1987–8, 68 per cent of cases submitted were withdrawn or settled before the hearing.

Similarly, a 'pre-hearing assessment' is sometimes used to settle a case at an early stage. This normally takes place if one party appears to have little or no chance of success. Either side can request a pre-hearing assessment but it is up to the tribunal to decide if it is appropriate in the circumstances. (The tribunal can also call a pre-hearing assessment if it sees fit. In 1987–8 36 per cent were initiated by the tribunal itself.)

Usually, only the person who has a case of little merit will attend at this stage (but the other side has a right to attend too if so desired). The case will be discussed and although the tribunal cannot reach a decision or dismiss a case at this point, it can, and frequently does, warn the person that if he proceeds he may be liable for the other person's costs. (Normally, at a full hearing both sides are responsible for their own costs although they may claim modest travelling and subsistence allowances.)

If the case goes to a full hearing, both parties will be sent a notice (IT4) 14 days before the date set. At the hearing – which is very flexible and informal – both the applicant and the defendant can address the tribunal and call witnesses and produce documentary evidence to support their statements. If either party believes a valuable witness may be reluctant to appear, they can apply to the court for a 'witness order' which requires that person to attend. A fine may be levied if he does not. Similarly, either side can ask the court to order the other to produce any documents that may be relevant; for example, an employee claiming unfair dismissal may request that his personnel records are produced by the employer.

During the hearing, the applicant and respondent can act on their own behalf – they will be given every assistance by the court. Alternatively, they may be represented by a solicitor, trade union official or even a friend. In 1986–7, 32 per cent of applicants and 45 per cent of respondents were legally represented with a further 20 per cent of applicants supported by a union representative. All in all, 65 per cent of applicants and 57 per cent of respondents were represented in some way.

After listening to and assessing the evidence, the tribunal will reach its decision. This – and their reasons – will often be given at the end of the hearing. Both parties will subsequently always be sent a statement re-stating the decision and explaining the reasons behind it.

In cases relating to claims of unfair dismissal, the tribunal may order that the applicant is either re-instated in his old job on the same terms and conditions or re-engaged in a similar job. The tribunal will, of course, take account of all circumstances: for example, the applicant may not want to work for the employer again or it may not be practicable for the employer to comply with such an order.

Alternatively, the tribunal may order the employer to give the employee financial compensation. This is subject to various maximum figures consisting of a basic award (based on the employee's age, service and pay) up to a maximum of £5,520, a compensatory award (based on the loss he has suffered because of the dismissal – effectively 'damages') of up to £8,925 and – in cases where the employer refuses to comply with a re-instatement or re-engagement order – an additional award up to £4,784 (1990 figures). Clearly unfair dismissal can prove costly for an employer. (Your attention is therefore drawn to the section of this book entitled 'Dismissing staff'.)

It is sometimes possible to appeal against a decision. The tribunal may review the case (and possibly amend their decision) if, and only if:

- an incorrect decision was reached because the tribunal made an error;
- either the applicant or respondent did not receive notification of the hearing;
- one of the parties or a person entitled to be heard was absent (perhaps through ill health);
- either side subsequently discovers new evidence;
- a review is needed 'in the interests of justice'.

A review will *not* take place simply because one side disagrees with the tribunal's decision.

The Employment Appeal Tribunal can hear appeals on 'points of law' only. An employer (or employee) contemplating this course of action should consult his solicitor first. Further appeals can be taken to the Court of Appeal (Court of Session in Scotland) and ultimately to the House of Lords.

Your local Department of Employment will supply a booklet 'Industrial Tribunals Procedure' (ITL 1) which you may find useful. There are organizations detailed in the Appendix which may provide further help and advice.

Key points

- By law, both employers and employees must give and receive certain minimum periods of notice if they want to terminate a contract of employment. It may be sensible to consider the points for and against agreeing to longer periods of notice.

- All small businesses will occasionally have to handle an employee who wants to leave. An exit interview should always be conducted to discover his reasons for resigning, resolve problems that might make him change his mind and identify areas for improvement that could help to avoid more resignations.

- To dismiss an employee fairly, an employer must have sufficient reason and should act reasonably at all times. Incapability, misconduct, redundancy, legal or any other substantial reason would be appropriate grounds so long as opportunities to improve were given, the alternatives to dismissal were looked at beforehand and so on. If not, it could be termed an unfair dismissal.

- Industrial tribunals are independent, judicial bodies which deal with complaints and settle disputes concerning employees' legal rights, mainly relating to claims of unfair dismissal. They can order an employer to re-instate or re-engage an employee in the same or a similar job and/or compensate him financially.

- It is important to remember that advice and guidance can be sought from the Department of Employment as and when required.

8

Employment law

Outline

Every small business owner and manager has to be aware of all
aspects of employment law. This chapter highlights some of
the key issues previously raised. It considers:

- calculating your staff needs;
- recruiting staff;
- training staff;
- employing staff;
- controlling staff;
- dealing with staff;
- ending employment.

In many ways, employment law has formed the backbone of this
book. Statutes have been referred to when appropriate, key points
made and sources of further reading and advice regularly given. A
separate chapter on law is therefore probably unnecessary. You can
simply turn to the appropriate section to discover the basic information you require. Nevertheless, it may be worthwhile taking each
chapter in turn and looking briefly at the most common employment
law questions posed by small business people.

This chapter takes the form of a series of short questions and
answers which will act as a quick summary of some of the more
important points and perhaps draw in a number of other, minor
points not previously mentioned.

You could assess whether you have a good working knowledge of
managing staff by answering each question yourself before looking
at the answer provided.

Calculating your staff needs

Q: What legal requirements should I consider when calculating staff needs?

A: You must avoid discriminating on the grounds of sex, marital status or race. Be especially careful when you draw up a person specification. Do not set criteria which may favour one group more than another. For further information, see 'Avoiding discrimination' or obtain copies of the Sex Discrimination Act 1975 or Race Relations Act 1976.

   If you employ more than twenty staff, at least 3 per cent of them should be disabled. Refer to 'Avoiding discrimination' or a copy of the Disabled Persons (Employment) Acts 1944 and 1958.

Recruiting staff

Q: What are the legal rights of job applicants?

A: Once again, you must be careful not to discriminate on the grounds of sex, marital status or race. Think carefully about the way you phrase adverts, pre-screen applicants and inter-view them. At every stage of the recruitment and selection process ask yourself a simple question: 'Am I discriminating?' (If you feel you are, follow this with a second question: 'How can I avoid discrimination?') See 'Avoiding discrimination', the Sex Discrimination Act 1975 and the Race Relations Act 1976.

Q: What details should be included in the written statement of the main terms of employment?

A: Employees who work for 16 hours per week or more (or for 8–16 hours each week for 5 years) must be given information about: the employer and employee's names, the job title, the date employment commenced, pay, hours, holidays, sickness, pensions, discipline, grievances and notice entitlement. These details should be supplied within 13 weeks of starting work.

Refer to 'Accepting the job offer' or the Employment Protection (Consolidation) Act 1978.

Training staff

Q: Are there any legal restrictions concerning the employee's personnel record that I need to know about?

A: The Data Protection Act was passed in 1984 to regulate the type and use of information held about individuals on computers. Data users must adhere to certain standards. For example: data should be fairly obtained, kept accurate and up to date and used for registered purposes only.

This Act does not cover manually kept data (card indexes etc.) and, as such, will be of little interest to many smaller businesses. Nevertheless, if you think it may be of relevance, obtain a copy of the Act.

Employing staff

Q: What exactly is a contract of employment?

A: It is simply an agreement of the terms and conditions that exist between you and your employee. Normally, it will be based on the previously mentioned written statement of the main terms of employment plus other written information provided in job adverts, offers of employment and staff reference documents. Verbal comments made – on the telephone, at an interview etc. – could be included too. See 'Contracts of employment' and the Employment Protection (Consolidation) Act 1978.

Q: How can a contract of employment be altered?

A: Changes should normally be made by agreement. Written confirmation of the change should be given to the employee within one month. Refer to the Employment Protection (Consolidation) Act 1978.

Q: How do the statutory employment rights differ between temporary, part-time and full-time staff?

A: It depends on each particular statutory right. Some apply to all employees regardless of length of service or hours worked (for example, every employee has a right not to be discriminated against because of his or her sex, race or marital status). Others will only apply if the employee works for a certain number of hours each week (usually 16 hours) or for a certain pèriod of time (perhaps 2 years). See the appropriate section for further information.

Q: What legal requirements should I consider concerning pay?

A: First, remember that employees who do the same or 'broadly similar' work should receive the same pay. Refer to 'Avoiding discrimination' and the Equal Pay Act 1970.

If you recognize a trade union, you may need to adhere to any pay agreements made. See 'Staff representation'.

You will need to deduct tax and national insurance contributions under the PAYE system. Refer to 'Pay and deductions' and the Wages Act 1986.

Employees who work for 16 hours or more each week (or 8–16 hours per week for 5 years) should be given an itemized pay statement. This must detail gross pay, fixed deductions, variable deductions and net pay. See 'Pay and deductions' and the Employment Protection (Consolidation) Act 1978.

You may also have to pay Statutory Sick pay or Statutory Maternity Pay if certain qualifying conditions are met. Refer to 'Statutory Sick Pay' and 'Maternity benefits'.

Q: When can an employee take time off work?

A: Apart from holiday entitlement (which must be detailed in the written statement of the main terms of employment), employees are entitled to reasonable paid time off for ante-natal care, to look for work when under notice of redundancy (if they have worked for you for 16 hours per week for 2 years) or to carry out trade union duties (if they are union officials or safety representatives).

In addition, they are also entitled to reasonable unpaid time off for public duties, jury service or union activities (if they are members of a recognized trade union).

See 'Holidays and time off' and the Employment Protection (Consolidation) Act 1978.

Q: Can I take out insurance to protect my business against claims brought by employees injured in the course of employment?

A: The Employers Liability (Compulsory Insurance) Act of 1969 states that employers *must* be insured against such claims. The policy must provide cover for up to £2 million for any one claim. The certificate must be clearly displayed where it can be seen by all your staff.

You should be aware of two exceptions though. You do not have to be insured against claims by close relatives. Nor do you have to take out this insurance if employees work in a private household.

Refer to your local insurance broker for advice. At the same time discuss taking out public liability insurance (a customer may be injured on your premises – perhaps through an employee's incompetence), professional indemnity insurance (you or your employees could offer a customer harmful or dangerous professional advice) and fidelity insurance (an employee may steal from you).

Controlling staff

Q: How should information about disciplinary, grievance and appeal rules and procedures be provided?

A: By law, this information should be detailed in the written statement of the main terms of employment *or* in staff reference documents (in which case reference must be made to them within the written statement). Whatever your choice, it is important that the rules and procedures are in writing, clearly understood and fair and reasonable. See 'Disciplinary procedure', 'Grievance procedure' and the Employment Protection (Consolidation) Act 1978.

Dealing with staff

Q: Do I have to negotiate with a trade union?

A: No, but it may be advisable to do so if the majority of your employees wish you to. Refer to 'Staff representation'.

Q: What are the rights of trade union members?

A: They have the right to belong to the union, participate in trade union activities at an appropriate time and have reasonable time off for trade union duties (paid) or activities (usually unpaid). They are also entitled not to be discriminated against because of their union membership, duties or activities. (See 'Staff representation'.)

Ending employment

Q: How much notice must I give an employee?

A: By law, employees who work for 16 hours or more each week (or 8–16 hours for 5 years) are entitled to a minimum statutory period of notice. For employment between one month and 2 years they must be given one week's notice. An extra week's notice must be provided for every complete year worked up to a maximum of 12 weeks. Refer to 'Giving notice' and the Employment Protection (Consolidation) Act 1978.

Q: How much notice should an employee give me?

A: Once an employee completes one month's service, you are entitled to one week's notice. This does not increase with service. See 'Giving notice' and the Employment Protection (Consolidation) Act 1978.

Q: Must these periods of notice always be adhered to?

A: No, they are simply the *minimum* statutory periods required by law. A contract of employment can specify longer periods. In addition, you should be aware that either party can waive their right to notice if they wish. Also, either party can terminate employment without notice if the behaviour of the other party warrants it. Refer to 'Dismissing staff' and the Employment Protection (Consolidation) Act 1978.

Q: What is a 'fair dismissal'?

A: To be 'fair', you must have 'sufficient reason' and have 'acted reasonably at all times'. Sufficient reason could include incapability, misconduct, legal reasons, redundancy or 'any other substantial reason'. To act reasonably you must – depending on the circumstances – give an employee every chance to improve, adhere to a fair disciplinary procedure and consider all the alternatives to dismissal. See 'Dismissing staff' and 'Disciplinary procedure'.

Q: What do I need to know about redundancy?

A: Important legal considerations include notifying the Department of Employment and any recognized trade union at least 30 days before the first redundancy is made (if ten or more employees are being made redundant), allowing employees (who have worked 16 hours per week for 2 years) paid time off to look for work and making redundancy payments according to age and length of employment (if qualifying conditions are met).

Q: What happens to my employee's rights if I sell my business?

A: Employees are entitled to continue on the same terms and conditions. All statutory rights are protected. Refer to the Department of Employment's booklet 'Employment Rights on the Transfer of an Undertaking'.

Q: What employment Acts do I need to know about?

A: You will need to have a basic understanding, not necessarily in great depth, of the following:
- Employment Protection (Consolidation) Act 1978.
- The Wages Act 1986.
- Sex Discrimination Act 1975.
- Race Relations Act 1976.
- Equal Pay Act 1970.
- Disabled Persons (Employment) Acts 1944 and 1958.
- Health and Safety at Work Act 1974.
- Data Protection Act 1984.

- Employers Liability (Compulsory Insurance) Act 1969.

Q: Where can I obtain copies of these Acts should I require detailed information?

A: Her Majesty's Stationery Office (HMSO) is the Government publisher. The Head Office is at St Crispins, Duke Street, Norwich, Norfolk NR3 1PD (0603) 622211.

Key points

- Every small business owner and manager must be fully aware of the legal requirements relating to calculating staff needs, recruiting, training, employing, controlling and dealing with staff. He also needs to understand the law concerning ending employment. It is vitally important that the law is adhered to at all times.
- As much information as possible must be obtained about current legislation. Her Majesty's Stationery Office will supply copies of appropriate Acts. Other books should be read (see 'Further reading'). Advisory organizations must be contacted.

Appendix: Sources of information

Advisory, Conciliation and Arbitration Service (ACAS)

Head Office:
11–12 St James Square
London SW1Y 4LA
(071–210 3000).

Alpha Tower
Suffolk Street Queensway
Birmingham B1 1TZ
(021–643 9911)

16 Park Place
Clifton
Bristol BS8 1JP
(0272 211921)

Phase 1
Ty Glas Road
Llanishen
Cardiff CF4 5PH
(0222 762636)

Franborough House
123 Bothwell Street
Glasgow G2 7JR
(041–204 2677)

Commerce House
St Alban's Place
Leeds LS2 8HH
(0532 431371)

Clifton House
83 Euston Road
London NW1 2RB
(071–388 5100)

Boulton House
17 Chorlton Street
Manchester M1 3HY
(061–228 3222)

Westgate House
Westgate Road
Newcastle upon Tyne NE1 1TJ
(0632 612191)

Association of the British Chambers of Commerce
Sovereign House
212 Shaftesbury Avenue
London WC2H 8EW
(071–240–5831)

Association of Independent Businesses
133 Copeland Road
London SE15 3SP
(071–277 5158)

British Institute of Management (BIM)
Management House
Cottingham Road
Corby
Northants NN17 1TT
(0536 204222)

BIM offers well-priced management information services, short courses and publications for its members. Non-members may also take advantage of the excellent facilities etc. at an appropriate extra cost.

British Insurance Brokers Association
Aldermary House
Queen Street
London EC4P 4JD
(071–248 4477)

Central Office of the Industrial Tribunals (England and Wales)
93 Ebury Bridge Road
London SW1W 8RE
(071–730 9161)

Central Office of the Industrial Tribunals (Scotland)
Saint Andrew House
141 West Nile Street
Glasgow G1 2RU
(041–331 1601)

These two Central Offices will put you in touch with the appropriate regional office.

Commission for Racial Equality
10–12 Allington Street
London SW1E 5EH
(071–828 7022)

Croner Publications Ltd
Croner House
London Road
Kingston upon Thames
Surrey KT2 6SR
(081–547 3333)

Croner publish a wide selection of loose leaf books on employment law and related matters of interest to small businesses. They are updated monthly or bi-monthly in most instances.

Department of Social Security
(Leaflets Unit)
PO Box 21
Stanmore
Middlesex HA17 1AY
A nationwide Social Security Advice Line for Employers also exists. Call 0800 393 539.

Employment Department
2 Duchess Place
Hagley Road
Birmingham B16 8NS
(021–456 1144)

Equal Opportunities Commission
Overseas House
Quay Street
Manchester M3 3HN
(061–833 9244)

Caerways House
Windsor Lane
Cardiff CF1 1LB
(0222 43552)

St Andrew House
141 West Nile Street
Glasgow G1 2RN
(041–332 8018)

Focus
Northside House
Mount Pleasant
Barnet
Herts EN4 9EB
(081–441 9300)

Future Perfect
Westminster House
2 Dean Stanley Street
London SW1P 3JP
(071–799 2702)

Health and Safety Executive
St Hugh's House
Trinity Road
Bootle L20 2QY
(051–951 4381)

Baynards House
1 Chepstow Place
London W2 4TF
(071–221 0416)

Broad Lane
Sheffield S3 7HQ
(0742 752539)

Her Majesty's Stationery Office
St Crispins
Duke Street
Norwich
Norfolk NR3 1PD
(0603 622211)

Institute of Personnel Management
IPM House
Camp Road
Wimbledon
London SW19 4UW
(081–946 9100)

Insurance Brokers Registration Council
15 St Helens Place
London EC3A 6DS
(071–588 4387)

National Chamber of Trade
Enterprise House
Henley on Thames
Oxon RG19 1TU
(0491 576161)

National Council for Voluntary Organizations
26 Bedford Square
London WC1B 3HU
(071–636 4066)

National Federation of Self Employed and Small Businesses Ltd
Head Office:
32 St Annes Road West
Lytham St Annes
Lancashire FY8 1NY
(0253 720911)

Unit 101c Argent Centre
60 Frederick Street

Birmingham B1 3HS
(021–236 6849)

11 Great George Street
Bristol BS1 5QY
(0272 276073)

Duke Street
Arcade Chambers
Duke Street Arcade
Cardiff CF1 2BA
(0222 398640)

34 Argyle Arcade
Glasgow G2 8BD
(041–221 0775)

35a Appletongate
Newark
Notts NG24 1JR
(0636 701311)

5 Norden House
39–41 Stowell Street
Newcastle upon Tyne NE1 4YB
(0632 324221)

National Out of School Alliance
Oxford House,
Derbyshire Street
London E2 6HG
(071–739 4787)

Open University
Walton Hall
Milton Keynes MK7 6AA
(0908 653473)

Oracle Teletext Ltd
See page 24

Pre-Retirement Association
Hogg Robinson House
42–62 Greyfriars Road
Reading
Berkshire RG1 1NN
(0734 583683)

Race Relations Employment Advisory Service
Birmingham:
14th Floor
Cumberland House
Birmingham B15 1TA
(021–631 3300 Ext. 201)
Leeds:
City House
Leeds LS1 4JH
(0532 438232 Ext. 2344)
London:
11 Belgrave Road
London SW1V 1RB
(071–834 6644)
Manchester:
Room 1713
Sunley Tower
Picadilly Plaza
Manchester M60 7JS
(061–832 9111 Ext. 5922)
Nottingham:
102 Lower Parliament Street
Nottingham NG1 1EH
(0602 581224)

Rural Development Commission
141 Castle Street
Salisbury
Wiltshire SP1 3TP
(0722 336255)

Small Firms Service
Dial 100 ask for 'Freefone Enterprise' (you will be connected free of charge) or write to one of the following centres:

Alpha Tower
Suffolk Street
Queensway
Birmingham B1 1TT

6th Floor
The Pithay
Bristol BS1 2NB

Carlyle House
Carlyle Road
Cambridge CB4 3DN

16 St David's House
Wood Street
Cardiff CF1 1ER

21 Bothwell Street
Glasgow G2 6NR

1 Park Row
City Square
Leeds LS1 5NR

Graeme House
Derby Square
Liverpool L2 7UJ

Ebury Bridge House
2–18 Ebury Bridge Road
London SW1W 8QD

3rd Floor
Royal Exchange Buildings
St Ann's Square
Manchester M2 7AH

Centro House
3 Cloth Market
Newcastle upon Tyne NE1 1EE

Severns House
20 Middle Pavement
Nottingham NG1 7DW

Abbey Hall
Abbey Square
Reading RG1 3BE

Society of Pension Consultants
Ludgate House
Ludgate Circus
London EC4A 2AB
(071–353 1688)

Training Agency
Moorfoot
Sheffield S1 4PQ
(0742 753275)

Glossary

British Rate and Data (BRAD) A monthly publication which provides in-depth information about United Kingdom media. Widely available in larger libraries.

classified advertisement A line-by-line advertisement beneath a heading such as 'Jobs', 'Situations Vacant' or 'Employment Opportunities'.

collective bargaining Negotiations which take place between an employer and a trade union representing the employer's workforce.

contract of employment An agreement of the terms and conditions of employment between an employer and an employee. Based on both verbal and written information, including the written statement of the main terms of employment.

curriculum vitae (CV) A document detailing a person's personal and career history. Useful for pre-screening job applicants.

direct discrimination Where one person is treated less favourably than another, usually because of sex, marital status or race.

display advertisement An advertisement within its own border, usually with a mix of typefaces to attract maximum attention.

distance learning Where training is carried out by means of correspondence courses, supported by audio and video tapes, television programmes and tutorial assistance. Also known as 'open learning'.

employee specification See Person specification.

exit interview An interview conducted with an employee planning to leave, to establish his reasons and identify weaknesses in the way staff are recruited and managed.

fair dismissal Whereby an employer has sufficient reason to terminate an employee's contract of employment *and* acts reasonably at all times.

gross misconduct Actions – such as abusive behaviour or assault – which will lead to immediate disciplinary action, even instant dismissal.

indirect discrimination Whereby requirements – for recruitment, training or promotion – are set which favour one group of employees more than another.

induction The process of installing a new employee into a job, hopefully as promptly and efficiently as possible.

industrial tribunal A judicial body set up to preside over complaints and employer–employee disputes concerning an employee's statutory rights.

itemized pay statement A statement issued to employees working at least 16 hours per week (or over 8 hours per week for 5 years) detailing the employee's gross wage, amount and purpose of deductions and net wage.

job analysis The process of collecting and assessing information about a particular job.

job description A document which outlines the main purpose and tasks of a job.

job specification See *Person Specification*.

minor misconduct Relatively modest misdemeanours – such as unsuitable dress or a lengthy lunchbreak – which might lead to a formal disciplinary procedure if repeated.

national insurance A state-run scheme whereby employers and employees (and the self-employed) have to pay a proportion of their earnings to the DSS.

off the job training Where employees are taught through a mix of lectures and discussions away from their work environment. Typically run by training specialists.

on the job training Whereby employees work alongside more experienced colleagues who show them what to do and constantly supervise them until they are capable of working well on their own.

open learning See *Distance learning*.

panel interview An interview with two or more interviewers facing a candidate.

pay as you earn A tax collection scheme whereby employers deduct tax and national insurance from employee's wages, forwarding it to the Inland Revenue. Commonly known as PAYE.

payment by results A payment system whereby earnings are partly linked to actual results, such as the number of goods produced.

person specification Also known as a job, personnel, or employee specification, this document outlines the skills, knowledge and experience needed to do a job successfully.

147

profit-sharing A system where earnings are partially related to company profits.

rate card Available from newspapers, magazines and radio stations, this card details their current advertising rates and other useful information about the market.

redundancy A situation which occurs when a job (or jobs) ceases to exist, perhaps because an employer no longer has sufficient work to offer all of his employees.

semi-display advertisement A display advert that is located below a classified heading.

serious misconduct Behaviour – such as continual, unauthorized lateness or absence – which will lead to disciplinary action, and even dismissal should it persist.

single column centimetre (s.c.c.) A basic unit of measurement used by newspapers and magazines to calculate advertising costs.

Statutory Maternity Pay (SMP) A state scheme run by employers through which pregnant employees obtain maternity pay before and after the birth as long as certain rules and procedures are adhered to.

Statutory Sick Pay (SSP) A state scheme operated by employers which entitles sick employees to sick pay for a limited period if various rules are met and procedures are followed.

summary dismissal Where an employer immediately terminates an employee's contract without notice due to the employee's gross misconduct.

tax allowance The amount of pay that can be earned in a tax year that is not subject to income tax.

taxable pay Those earnings which are subject to income tax.

time rate A payment system where earnings are related solely to the number of hours worked.

unfair dismissal Whereby an employer terminates an employee's contract of employment without sufficient reason and/or without acting in a reasonable manner at all times.

works committee A committee consisting of employees (representing the workforce) and management (on behalf of the company) which meets regularly to discuss work-related issues.

written statement of the main terms of employment A document highlighting the key points of an employee's contract of employment.

Further reading

In addition to the many booklets and leaflets referred to throughout the text, the following books are highly recommended.

General books

Croner's Reference Book for the Self Employed and Smaller Business (Kingston upon Thames, Croner Publications).

Croner's Reference Book for Employers (Kingston upon Thames, Croner Publications).

Armstrong, Michael, *A Handbook of Personnel Management Practice*, 2nd edn (London, Kogan Page, 1984).

Cuming, Maurice W., *The Theory and Practice of Personnel Management*, 6th edn (Oxford, Heinemann, 1988).

Chapter 1   Calculating your staff needs

Manpower Planning: Management Checklist No. 6 (Corby, British Institute of Management, 1988).

Pettman, Barrie O., *Manpower Planning Workbook*, 2nd edn (Aldershot, Gower, 1984).

Chapter 2   Recruiting staff

Fletcher, John, *Effective Interviewing*, 3rd edn (London, Kogan Page, 1988).

Maitland, Iain, *How to Win at Interviews* (London, Business Books, 1989).

Maitland, Iain, *Running a Successful Advertising Campaign* (London, Telegraph Publications, 1988).

Quinn, Patrick, *The Secrets of Successful Low Budget Advertising* (Oxford, Heinemann, 1988).

Ray, Maurice, *Recruitment Advertising* (London, Institute of Personnel Management, 1980).

Shackleton, Viv, *How to Pick People for Jobs* (London, Fontana, 1989).

Chapter 3 Training staff

Formal Induction Programmes: Management Checklist No. 7 (Corby, British Institute of Management, 1989).
Rae, Leslie, *The Skills of Training* (Aldershot, Gower, 1983).

Chapter 4 Employing staff

Armstrong, Michael and Murlis, H., *A Handbook of Salary Administration* (London, Kogan Page, 1980).
Smith, Ian, *Incentive Schemes: People and Profits* (Kingston upon Thames, Croner Publications, 1989).
Thompson, Mary, *Employment for Disabled People* (London, Kogan Page, 1980).

Chapter 5 Controlling staff

Croner's Guide to Discipline (Kingston upon Thames, Croner Publications, 1982).
Decision Making: Management Checklist No. 19 (Corby, British Institute of Management, 1985).
Disciplinary Procedure and Interviews: Management Checklist No. 87 (Corby, British Institute of Management, 1987).

Chapter 6 Dealing with staff

Bowers, John and Duggan, Michael, *The Modern Law of Strikes*, 2nd edn (Kingston upon Thames, Croner Publications, 1989).
Evans, Desmond W., *People, Communication and Organisations* (London, Pitman, 1986).
Evans, R. S., *An Employer's Guide to Tax Efficient Fringe Benefits* (Kingston upon Thames, Croner Publications, 1989).
Goodworth, Clive, *The Secrets of Successful Leadership and People Management* (Oxford, Heinemann, 1990).
Goodworth, Clive, *The Secrets of Successful Staff Appraisal and Counselling* (Oxford, Heinemann, 1989).
Kieffer, George David, *The Strategy of Meetings* (London, Piatkus, 1990).
McCann, Dick, *How to Influence Others at Work* (Oxford, Heinemann, 1989).

Oldfield, Maurice (ed.), *The PMI Guide to Pensions* (Oxford, Heinemann, 1988).

Scott, Bill, *The Skills of Communicating* (Aldershot, Gower, 1986).

Spill, Ron, *Practical Pensions and Related Benefits* (Kingston upon Thames, Croner Publications, 1989).

Toulson, Norman, *Managing Pension Schemes* (Aldershot, Gower, 1986).

Chapter 7   Ending employment

Kemp, F., *Focus on Redundancy* (London, Kogan Page, 1980).

Toulson, Norman, *Preparing Staff for Retirement* (Aldershot, Gower, 1987).

Chapter 8   Employment law

Croner's Employment Law (Kingston upon Thames, Croner Publications).

Bowers, John, *A Practical Approach to Employment Law*, 2nd edn (Kingston upon Thames, Croner Publications, 1989).

Clayton, Patricia, *Law for the Small Business*, 5th edn (London, Kogan Page, 1987).

Janner, Greville, *Janner's Personnel Law* (Aldershot, Gower, 1989).

Whincup, Michael, *Modern Employment Law*, 6th edn (Oxford, Heinemann, 1988).

Books published by Croner Publications Ltd and the British Institute of Management can be purchased direct from the addresses given in the Appendix. The other books listed should be available through your local bookshop or library.

Barclays Guides for the Small Business

The following titles are available in this series:

Wilson: *Financial Management for the Small Business* 0 631 17254 8 ☐
Rogers: *Marketing for the Small Business* 0 631 17247 5 ☐
Aziz: *Computing for the Small Business* 0 631 17256 4 ☐
Wilson: *International Trade for the Small Business* 0 631 17252 1 ☐
Maitland: *Managing Staff for the Small Business* 0 631 17482 6 ☐
Lloyd: *Law for the Small Business* 0 631 17349 8 ☐
Stanworth & Smith: *Franchising for the Small Business* 0 631 17498 2 ☐
Gray: *Managing Growth in the Small Business* 0 631 17249 1 ☐
Gammon: *Buying and Selling for the Small Business* 0 631 17528 8 ☐
All titles are £6.95 each.

You can order through your local bookseller or, in case of difficulty, direct from the publisher using this order form. Please indicate the quantity of books you require in the boxes above and complete the details form below. The publisher will be pleased to negotiate a discount for orders of more than 20 copies of one title.

Payment
Please add £2.50 to payment to cover p&p.

☐ Please charge my Mastercard/Visa/American Express account

card number ☐☐☐☐☐☐☐☐☐☐☐☐☐☐☐☐☐

Expiry date _____

Signature _____
          (credit card orders must be signed to be valid)

☐ I enclose a cheque for £_____ made payable to **Marston Book Services Ltd**

(PLEASE PRINT)
Name _____

Address _____

_____

_____ Postcode _____

Tel No _____

Signature _____ Date _____

Please return the completed form with remittance to:
Department DM, Basil Blackwell Ltd
108 Cowley Road, Oxford OX4 1JF, UK
or telephone your credit card order on 0865 791155.

Goods will be despatched within 14 days of receipt of order. Data supplied may be used to inform you about other Basil Blackwell publications in relevant fields.
Registered in England No. 180277 Basil Blackwell Ltd.